Contents

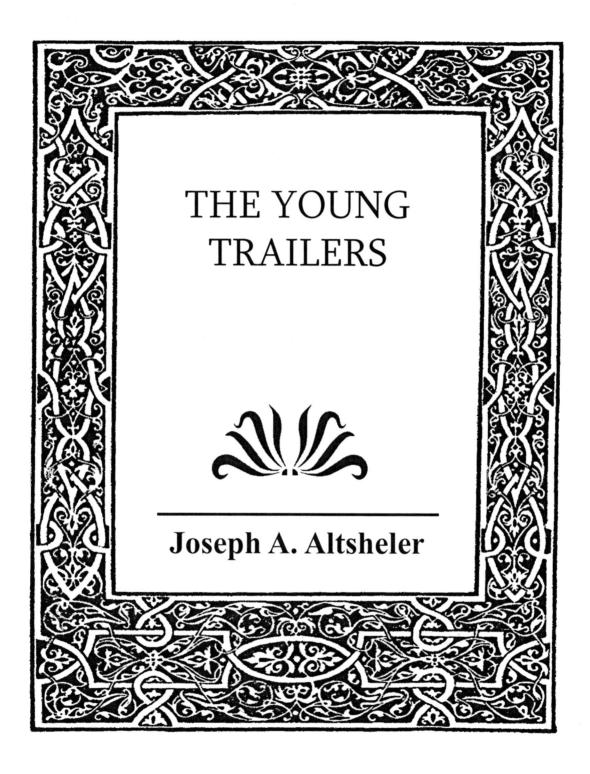

THE YOUNG TRAILERS

Joseph A. Altsheler

THE YOUNG TRAILERS

BY

JOSEPH A. ALTSHELER

CHAPTER I
INTO THE UNKNOWN

IT was a white caravan that looked down from the crest of the mountains upon the green wilderness, called by the Indians, Kain-tuck-ee. The wagons, a score or so in number, were covered with arched canvas, bleached by the rains, and, as they stood there, side by side, they looked like a snowdrift against the emerald expanse of forest and foliage.

The travelers saw the land of hope, outspread before them, a wide sweep of rolling country, covered with trees and canebrake, cut by streams of clear water, flowing here and there, and shining in the distance, amid the green, like threads of silver wire. All gazed, keen with interest and curiosity, because this unknown land was to be their home, but none was more eager than Henry Ware, a strong boy of fifteen who stood in front of the wagons beside the guide, Tom Ross, a tall, lean man the color of well-tanned leather, who would never let his rifle go out of his hand, and who had Henry's heartfelt admiration, because he knew so much about the woods and wild animals, and told such strange and absorbing tales of the great wilderness that now lay before them.

But any close observer who noted Henry Ware would always have looked at him a second time. He was tall and muscled beyond his years, and when he walked his figure showed a certain litheness and power like that of the forest bred. His gaze was rapid, penetrating and inclusive, but never furtive. He seemed to fit into the picture of the wilderness, as if he had taken a space reserved there for him, and had put himself in complete harmony with all its details.

The long journey from their old home in Maryland had been a source of unending variety and delight to Henry. There had been no painful partings. His mother and his brother and young sister were in the fourth wagon from the right, and his father stood beside it. Farther on in the same company were his uncles and aunts, and many of the old neighbors. All had come together. It was really the removal of a village from an old land to a new one, and with the familiar faces of kindred and friends around them, they were not lonely in strange regions, though mountains frowned and dark forests lowered.

It was to Henry a return rather than a removal. He almost fancied that in some far-off age he had seen all these things before. The forests and the mountains beckoned in friendly fashion; they had no terrors, for even their secrets lay open before him. He seemed to breathe a newer and keener air than that of the old land left behind, and his mind expanded with the thought of fresh pleasures to come. The veteran guide, Ross, alone observed how the boy learned, through intuition, ways of the wilderness that others achieved only by hard experience.

They had met fair weather, an important item in such a journey, and there had been no illness, beyond trifling ailments quickly cured. As they traveled slowly and at their ease, it took them a long time to pass through the settled regions. This part of the journey did not interest Henry so much. He was eager for the forests and the great wilderness where his fancy had already gone before. He wanted to see deer and bears and buffaloes, trees bigger than any that grew in Maryland, and mountains and mighty rivers. But they left the settlements behind at last, and came to the unbroken forest. Here he found his hopes fulfilled. They were on the first slopes of the mountains that divide Virginia from Kentucky, and the bold, wild nature of the country pleased him. He had never seen mountains before, and he felt the dignity and grandeur of the peaks.

Sometimes he went on ahead with Tom Ross, the guide, his chosen friend, and then he considered himself, in very truth, a man, or soon to become one, because he was now exploring the unknown, leading the way for a caravan--and there could be no more important duty. At such moments he listened to the talk of the guide who taught the lesson that in the wilderness it was always important to see and to listen, a thing however that Henry already knew instinctively. He learned the usual sounds of the woods, and if there was any new noise he would see what made it. He studied, too, the habits of the beasts and birds. As for fishing, he found that easy. He could cut a rod with his clasp knife, tie a string to the end of it and a bent pin to the end of a string, and with this rude tackle he could soon catch in the mountain creeks as many fish as he wanted.

Henry liked the nights in the mountains; in which he did not differ from his fellow-travelers. Then the work of the day was done; the wagons were drawn up in a half circle, the horses and the oxen were resting or grazing under the trees, and, as they needed fires for warmth as well as cooking, they built them high and long, giving room for all in front of the red coals if they wished. The forest was full of fallen brushwood, as dry as tinder, and Henry helped gather it. It pleased him to see the flames rise far up, and to hear them crackle as they ate into the heart of the boughs. He liked to see their long red shadows fall across the leaves and grass, peopling the dark forest with fierce wild animals; he would feel all the cosier within the scarlet rim of the firelight. Then the men would tell stories, particularly Ross, the guide, who had wandered much and far in Kentucky. He said that it was a beautiful land. He spoke of the noble forests of beech and oak and hickory and maple, the dense canebrake, the many rivers, and the great Ohio that received them all--the Beautiful River, the Indians called it--and the game, with which forests and open alike swarmed, the deer, the elk, the bear, the panther and the buffalo. Now and then, when the smaller children were asleep in the wagons and the larger ones were nodding before the fires, the men would sink their voices and speak of a subject which made them all look very grave indeed. It sounded like Indians, and the men more than once glanced at their rifles and powderhorns.

But the boy, when he heard them, did not feel afraid. He knew that savages of the most dangerous kind often came into the forests of Kentucky, whither they were going, but he thrilled rather than shivered at the thought. Already he seemed to have the knowledge that he would be a match for them at any game they wished to play.

Henry usually slept very soundly, as became a boy who was on his feet nearly all day, and who did his share of the work; but two or three times he awoke far in the night, and, raising himself up in the wagon, peeped out between the canvas cover and the wooden body. He saw a very black night in which the trees looked as thin and ghostly as shadows, and smoldering fires, beside which two men rifle on shoulder, always watched. Often he had a wish to watch with them, but he said nothing, knowing that the others would hold him too young for the task.

But to-day he felt only joy and curiosity. They were now on the crest of the last mountain ridge and before them lay the great valley of Kentucky; their future home. The long journey was over. The men took off their hats and caps and raised a cheer, the women joined through sympathy and the children shouted, too, because their fathers and mothers did so, Henry's voice rising with the loudest.

A slip of a girl beside Henry raised an applauding treble and he smiled protectingly at her. It was Lucy Upton, two years younger than himself, slim and tall, dark-blue eyes looking from under broad brows, and dark-brown curls, lying thick and close upon a shapely head.

"Are you not afraid?" she asked.

"Afraid of what?" replied Henry Ware, disdainfully.

"Of the forests over there in Kentucky. They say that the savages often come to kill."

"We are too strong. I do not fear them."

He spoke without any vainglory, but in the utmost confidence. She glanced covertly at him. He seemed to her strong and full of resource. But she would not show her admiration.

They passed from the mountain slope into a country which now sank away in low, rolling hills like the waves of the sea and in which everything grew very beautiful. Henry had never seen such trees in the East. The beech, the elm, the hickory and the maple reached gigantic proportions, and wherever the shade was not too dense the grass rose heavy and rank. Now and then they passed thickets of canebrake, and once, at the side of a stream, they came to a salt "lick." It was here that a fountain spouted from the base of a hill, and, running only a few feet, emptied into a creek. But its waters were densely impregnated with salt, and all around its banks the soft soil was trodden with hundreds of footsteps.

"The wild beasts made these," said the guide to Henry. "They come here at night: elk, deer, buffalo, wolves, and all the others, big and little, to get the salt. They drink the water and they lick up the salt too from the ground."

A fierce desire laid hold of the boy at these words. He had a small rifle of his own, which however he was not permitted to carry often. But he wanted to take it and lie beside the pool at night when the game came down to drink. The dark would have no terrors for him, nor would he need companionship. He knew what to do, he could stay in the bush noiseless and motionless for hours, and he would choose only the finest of the deer and the bear. He could see himself drawing the bead, as a great buck came down in the shadows to the fountain and he thrilled with pleasure at the thought. Each new step into the wilderness seemed to bring him nearer home.

Their stay beside the salt spring was short, but the next night they built the fire higher than ever because just after dark they heard the howling of wolves, and a strange, long scream, like the shriek of a woman, which the men said was the cry of a panther. There was no danger, but the cries sounded lonesome and terrifying, and it took a big fire to bring back gayety.

Henry had not yet gone to bed, but was sitting in his favorite place beside the guide, who was calmly smoking a pipe, and he felt the immensity of the wilderness. He understood why the people in this caravan clung so closely to each other. They were simply a big family, far away from anybody else, and the woods, which curved around them for so many hundreds of miles, held them together.

The men talked more than usual that night, but they did not tell stories; instead they asked many questions of the guide about the country two days' journey farther on, which, Ross said, was so good, and it was agreed among them that they should settle there near the banks of a little river.

"It's the best land I ever saw," said Ross, "an' as there's lots of cane-brake it won't be bad to clear up for farmin'. I trapped beaver in them parts two years ago, an' I know."

This seemed to decide the men, and the women, too, for they had their share in the council. The long journey was soon to end, and all looked pleased, especially the women. The great question settled, the men lighted their pipes and smoked a while, in silence, before the blazing fires. Henry watched them and wished that he too was a man and could take part in these evening talks. He was excited by the knowledge that their journey was to end so soon, and he longed to see the valley in which they were to build their homes. He climbed into the wagon at last but he could not sleep. His beloved rifle, too, was lying near him, and once he reached out his hand and touched it.

The men, by and by, went to the wagons or, wrapping themselves in blankets, slept before the flames. Only two remained awake and on guard. They sat on logs near the outskirts of the camp and held their rifles in their hands.

Henry dropped the canvas edge and sought sleep, but it would not come. Too many thoughts were in his mind. He was trying to imagine the beautiful valley, described by Ross, in which they were to build their houses. He lifted the canvas again after a while and saw that the fires had sunk lower than ever. The two men were still sitting on the logs and leaning lazily against upthrust boughs. The wilderness around them was very black, and twenty yards away, even the outlines of the trees were lost in the darkness.

Henry's sister who was sleeping at the other end of the wagon awoke and cried for water. Mr. Ware raised himself sleepily, but Henry at once sprang up and offered to get it. "All right," Mr. Ware said.

Henry quickly slipped on his trousers and taking the tin cup in his hand climbed out of the wagon. He was in his bare feet, but like other pioneer boys he scorned shoes in warm weather, and stubble and pebbles did not trouble him.

The camp was in a glade and the spring was just at the edge of the woods--they stopped at night only by the side of running water, which was easy to find in this region. Near the spring some of the horses and two of the oxen were tethered to stout saplings. As Henry approached, a horse neighed, and he noticed that all of them were pulling on their ropes. The two careless guards were either asleep or so near it that they took no notice of what was passing, and Henry, unwilling to call their attention for fear he might seem too forward, walked among the animals, but was still unable to find the cause of the trouble. He knew everyone by name and nature, and they knew him, for they had been comrades on a long journey, and he patted their backs and rubbed their noses and tried to soothe them. They became a little quieter, but he could not remain any longer with them because his sister was waiting at the wagon for the water. So he went to the spring and, stooping down, filled his cup.

When Henry rose to his full height, his eyes happened to be turned toward the forest, and there, about seven or eight feet from the ground, and not far from him he saw two coals of fire. He was so startled that the cup trembled in his hand, and drops of water fell splashing back into the spring. But he stared steadily at the red points, which he now noticed were moving slightly from side to side, and presently he saw behind them the dim outlines of a long and large body. He knew that this must be a panther. The habits of all the wild animals, belonging to this region, had been described to him so minutely by Ross that he was sure he could not be mistaken. Either it was a very hungry or a very ignorant panther to hover so boldly around a camp full of men and guns.

The panther was crouched on a bough of a tree, as if ready to spring, and Henry was the nearest living object. It must be he at whom the great tawny body would be launched. But as a minute passed and the panther did not move, save to sway gently, his courage rose, especially when he remembered a saying of Ross that it was the natural impulse of all wild animals to run from man. So he began to back away, and he heard behind him the horses trampling about in alarm. The lazy guards still dozed and all was quiet at the wagons. Now Henry recalled some knowledge that he had learned from Ross and he made a resolve. He would show, at a time, when it was needed, what he really could do. He dropped his cup, rushed to the fire, and picked up a long brand, blazing at one end.

Swinging his torch around his head until it made a perfect circle of flame he ran directly toward the panther, uttering a loud shout as he ran. The animal gave forth his woman's cry, this time a shriek of terror, and leaping from the bough sped with cat-like swiftness into the forest.

All the camp was awake in an instant, the men springing out of the wagons, gun in hand, ready for any trouble. When they saw only a boy, holding a blazing torch above his head, they were disposed to grumble, and the two sleepy guards, seeking an excuse for themselves, laughed outright at the tale that Henry told. But Mr. Ware believed in the truth of his son's words, and the guide, who quickly examined the ground near the tree, said there could be no doubt that Henry had really seen the panther, and had not been tricked by his imagination. The great tracks of the beast were plainly visible in the soft earth.

"Pushed by hunger, an' thinking there was no danger, he might have sprung on one of our colts or a calf," said Ross, "an' no doubt the boy with his ready use of a torch has saved us from a loss. It was a brave thing for him to do."

But Henry took no pride in their praise. It was no part of his ambition merely to drive away a panther, instead he had the hunter's wish to kill him. He would be worthy of the wilderness.

Henry despite his lack of pride found the world very beautiful the next day. It was a fair enough scene. Nature had done her part, but his joyous mind gave to it deeper and more vivid colors. The wind was blowing from the south, bringing upon its breath the odor of wild flowers, and all the forest was green with the tender green of young spring. The cotton-tailed hares that he called rabbits ran across their path. Squirrels talked to one another in the tree tops, and defiantly threw the shells of last year's nuts at the passing travelers. Once they saw a stag bending down to drink at a brook, and when the forest king beheld them he raised his head, and merely stared at these strange new invaders of the wilds. Henry admired his beautiful form and splendid antlers nor would he have fired at him had it even been within orders. The deer gazed at them a few moments, and then, turning and tossing his head, sped away through the forest.

All that he saw was strange and grand to Henry, and he loved the wilderness. About noon he and Ross went back to the wagons and that night they encamped on the crest of a range of low and grassy hills. This was the rim of the valley that they had selected on the guide's advice as their future home, and the little camp was full of the liveliest interest in the morrow, because it is a most eventful thing, when you are going to choose a place which you intend shall be your home all the rest of your days. So the men and women sat late around the fires and even boys of Henry's age were allowed to stay up, too, and listen to the plans which all the grown people were making. Theirs had not been a hard journey, only long and tedious--though neither to Henry--and now that its end was at hand, work must be begun. They would have homes to build and a living to get from the ground.

"Why, I could live under the trees; I wouldn't want a house," whispered Henry to the guide, "and when I needed anything to eat, I'd kill game."

"A hunter might do that," replied Ross, "but we're not all hunters an' only a few of us can be. Sometimes the game ain't standin' to be shot at just when you want it, an' as for sleepin' under the trees it's all very fine in summer, if it don't rain, but 'twould be just a least bit chilly in winter when the big snows come as they do sometimes more'n a foot deep. I'm a hunter myself, an' I've slept under trees an' in caves, an' on the sheltered side of hills, but when the weather's cold give me for true comfort a wooden floor an' a board roof. Then I'll bargain to sleep to the king's taste."

But Henry was not wholly convinced. He felt in himself the power to meet and overcome rain or cold or any other kind of weather.

Everybody in the camp, down to the tiniest child, was awake the next morning by the time the first bar of gray in the east betokened the coming day. Henry was fully dressed, and saw the sun rise in a magnificent burst of red and gold over the valley that was to be their valley. The whole camp beheld the spectacle. They had reached the crest of the hill the evening before, too late to get a view and they were full of the keenest curiosity.

It was now summer, but, having been a season of plenteous rains, grass and foliage were of the most vivid and intense green. They were entering one of the richest portions of Kentucky, and the untouched soil was luxuriant with fertility. As a pioneer himself said: "All they had to do was to tickle it with a hoe, and it laughed into a harvest." There was the proof of its strength in the grass and the trees. Never before had the travelers seen oaks and beeches of such girth or elms and hickories of such height. The grass was high and thick and the canebrake was so dense that passage through it seemed impossible. Down the center of the valley, which was but one of many, separated from each other by low easy hills, flowed a little river, cleaving its center like a silver blade.

It was upon this beautiful prospect that the travelers saw the sun rise that morning and all their troubles and labors rolled away. Even the face of Mr. Ware who rarely yielded to enthusiasm kindled at the sight and, lifting his hand, he made with it a circle that described the valley.

"There," he said. "There is our home waiting for us."

"Hurrah!" cried Henry, flinging aloft his cap. "We've come home."

Then the wagon train started again and descended into the valley, which in very truth and fact was to be "home."

CHAPTER II
THE FIRST GREAT EXPLOIT

THEY found the valley everything in beauty and fertility that Ross had claimed for it, and above all it had small "openings," that is, places where the trees did not grow. This was very important to the travelers, as the labor of cutting down the forest was immense, and even Henry knew that they could not live wholly in the woods, as both children and crops must have sunshine to make them grow. The widest of these open spaces about a half mile from the river, they selected as the site of their new city to which they gave the name of Wareville in honor of their leader. A fine brook flowed directly through the opening, but Ross said it would be a good place, too, to sink a well.

It was midsummer now and the period of dry weather had begun. So the travelers were very comfortable in their wagon camp while they were making their new town ready to be lived in. Both for the sake of company and prudence they built the houses in a close cluster. First the men, and most of them were what would now be called jacks-of-all-trades, felled trees, six or eight inches in diameter, and cut them into logs, some of which were split down the center, making what are called puncheons; others were only nicked at the ends, being left in the rough, that is, with the bark on.

The round logs made the walls of their houses. First, the place where the house was to be built was chosen. Next the turf was cut off and the ground smoothed away. Then they "raised" the logs, the nicked ends fitting together at the corner, the whole inclosing a square. Everybody helped "raise" each house in turn, the men singing "hip-hip-ho!" as they rolled the heavy logs into position.

A place was cut out for a window and fastened with a shutter and a larger space was provided in the same manner for a door. They made the floor out of the puncheons, turned with the smooth side upward, and the roof out of rough boards, sawed from the trees. The chimney was built of earth and stones, and a great flat stone served as the fireplace. Some of the houses were large enough to have two rooms, one for the grown folks and one for the children, and Mr. Ware's also had a little lean-to or shed which served as a kitchen.

It seemed at first to Henry, rejoicing then in the warm, sunny weather, that they were building in a needlessly heavy and solid fashion. But when he thought over it a while he remembered what Ross said about the winters and deep snows of this new land. Indeed the winters in Kentucky are often very cold and sometimes for certain periods are quite as cold as those of New York or New England.

When the little town was finished at last it looked both picturesque and comfortable, a group of about thirty log houses, covering perhaps an acre of ground. But the building labors of the pioneers did not stop here. Around all these houses they put a triple palisade, that is three rows of stout, sharpened stakes, driven deep into the ground and rising full six feet above it. At intervals in this palisade were circular holes large enough to admit the muzzle of a rifle.

They built at each corner of the palisade the largest and strongest of their houses,--two-story structures of heavy logs, and Henry noticed that the second story projected over the first. Moreover, they made holes in the edge of the floor overhead so that one could look down through them upon anybody who stood by the outer wall. Ross went up into the second story of each of the four buildings, thrust the muzzle of his rifle into every one of the holes in turn, and then looked satisfied. "It is well done," he said. "Nobody can shelter himself against the wall from the fire of defenders up here."

These very strong buildings they called their blockhouses, and after they finished them they dug a well in the corner of the inclosed ground, striking water at a depth of twenty feet. Then their main labors were finished, and each family now began to furnish its house as it would or could.

It was not all work for Henry while this was going on, and some of the labor itself was just as good as play. He was allowed to go considerable distances with Ross, and these journeys were full of novelty. He was a boy who came to places which no white boy had ever seen before. It was hard for him to realize that it was all so new. Behold a splendid grove of oaks! he was its discoverer. Here the little river dropped over a cliff of ten feet; his eyes were the first to see the waterfall. From this high hill the view was wonderful; he was the first to enjoy it. Forest, open and canebrake alike were swarming with game, and he saw buffaloes, deer, wild turkeys, and multitudes of rabbits and squirrels. Unaccustomed yet to man, they allowed the explorers to come near.

Ross and Henry were accompanied on many of these journeys by Shif'less Sol Hyde. Sol was a young man without kith or kin in the settlement, and so, having nobody but himself to take care of, he chose to roam the country a great portion of the time. He was fast acquiring a skill in forest life and knowledge of its ways second only to that of Ross, the guide. Some of the men called Sol lazy, but he defended himself.

"The good God made different kinds of people and they live different kinds of lives," said he. "Mine suits me and harms nobody." Ross said he was right, and Sol became a hunter and scout for the settlement.

There was no lack of food. They yet had a good supply of the provisions brought with them from the other side of the mountains, but they saved them for a possible time of scarcity. Why should they use this store when they could kill all the game they needed within a mile of their own house smoke? Now Henry tasted the delights of buffalo tongue and beaver tail, venison, wild turkey, fried squirrel, wild goose, wild duck and a dozen kinds of fish. Never did a boy have more kinds of meat, morning, noon, and night. The forest was full of game, the fish were just standing up in the river and crying to be caught, and the air was sometimes dark with wild fowl. Henry enjoyed it. He was always hungry. Working and walking so much, and living in the open air every minute of his life, except when he was eating or sleeping, his young and growing frame demanded much nourishment, and it was not denied.

At last the great day came when he was allowed to kill a deer if he could. Both Ross and Shif'less Sol had interceded for him. "The boy's getting big and strong an' it's time he learned," said Ross. "His hand's steady enough an' his eye's good enough already," said Shif'less Sol, and his father agreeing with them told them to take him and teach him.

Two miles away, near the bank of the river, was a spring to which the game often came to drink, and for this spring they started a little while before sundown, Henry carrying his rifle on his shoulder, and his heart fluttering. He felt his years increase suddenly and his figure expand with equal abruptness. He had become a man and he was going forth to slay big game. Yet despite his new manhood the blood would run to his head and he felt his nerves trembling. He grasped his precious rifle more firmly and stole a look out of the corner of his eye at its barrel as it lay across his left shoulder. Though a smaller weapon it was modeled after the famous Western rifle, which, with the ax, won the wilderness. The stock was of hard maple wood delicately carved, and the barrel was comparatively long, slender, and of blue steel. The sights were as fine-drawn as a hair. When Henry stood the gun beside himself, it was just as tall as he. He carried, too, a powderhorn, and the horn, which was as white as snow, was scraped so thin as to be transparent, thus enabling its owner to know just how much powder it contained, without taking the trouble of pouring it out. His bullets and wadding he carried in a small leather pouch by his side.

When they reached the spring the sun was still a half hour high and filled the west with a red glow. The forest there was tinted by it, and seen thus in the coming twilight with those weird crimsons and scarlets showing through it, the wilderness looked very lonely and desolate. An ordinary boy, at the coming of night would have been awed, if alone, by the stillness of the great unknown spaces, but it found an answering chord in Henry.

"Wind's blowin' from the west," said Sol, and so they went to the eastern side of the spring, where they lay down beside a fallen log at a fair distance. There was another log, much closer to the spring, but Ross conferring aside with Sol chose the farther one. "We want to teach the boy how to shoot an' be of some use to himself, not to slaughter," said Ross. Then the three remained there, a long time, and noiseless. Henry was learning early one of the first great lessons of the forest, which is silence. But he knew that he could have learned this lesson alone. He already felt himself superior in some ways to Ross and Sol, but he liked them too well to tell them so, or to affect even equality in the lore of the wilderness.

The sun went down behind the Western forest, and the night came on, heavy and dark. A light wind began to moan among the trees. Henry heard the faint bubble of the water in the spring, and saw beside him the forms of his two comrades. But they were so still that they might have been dead. An hour passed and his eyes growing more used to the dimness, he saw better. There was still nothing at the spring, but by and by Ross put his hand gently upon his arm, and Henry, as if by instinct, looked in the right direction. There at the far edge of the forest was a deer, a noble stag, glancing warily about him.

The stag was a fine enough animal to Ross and Sol, but to Henry's unaccustomed eyes he seemed gigantic, the mightiest of his kind that ever walked the face of the earth.

The deer gazed cautiously, raising his great head, until his antlers looked to Henry like the branching boughs of a tree. The wind was blowing toward his hidden foes, and brought him no omen of coming danger. He stepped into the open and again glanced around the circle. It seemed to Henry that he was staring directly into the deer's eyes, and could see the fire shining there.

"Aim at that spot there by the shoulder, when he stoops down to drink," said Ross in the lowest of tones.

Satisfied now that no enemy was near, the stag walked to the spring. Then he began to lower slowly the great antlers, and his head approached the water. Henry slipped the barrel of his rifle across the log and looked down the sights. He was seized with a tremor, but Ross and Shif'less Sol, with a magnanimity that did them credit, pretended not to notice it. The boy soon mastered the feeling, but then, to his great surprise, he was attacked by another emotion. Suddenly he began to have pity, and a fellow-feeling for the stag. It, too, was in the great wilderness, rejoicing in the woods and the grass and the running streams and had done no harm. It seemed sad that so fine a life should end, without warning and for so little.

The feeling was that of a young boy, the instinct of one who had not learned to kill, and he suppressed it. Men had not yet thought to spare the wild animals, or to consider them part of a great brotherhood, least of all on the border, where the killing of game was a necessity. And so Henry, after a moment's hesitation, the cause of which he himself scarcely knew, picked the spot near the shoulder that Ross had mentioned, and pulled the trigger.

The stag stood for a moment or two as if dazed, then leaped into the air and ran to the edge of the woods, where he pitched down head foremost. His body quivered for a little while and then lay still.

Henry was proud of his marksmanship, but he felt some remorse, too, when he looked upon his victim. Yet he was eager to tell his father and his young sister and brother of his success. They took off the pelt and cut up the deer. A part of the haunch Henry ate for dinner and the antlers were fastened over the fireplace, as the first important hunting trophy won by the eldest son of the house.

Henry did not boast much of his triumph, although he noticed with secret pride the awe of the children. His best friend, Paul Cotter, openly expressed his admiration, but Braxton Wyatt, a boy of his own age, whom he did not like, sneered and counted it as nothing. He even cast doubt upon the reality of the deed, intimating that perhaps Ross or Sol had fired the shot, and had allowed Henry to claim the credit.

Henry now felt incessantly the longing for the wilderness, but, for the present, he helped his father furnish their house. It was too late to plant crops that year, nor were the qualities of the soil yet altogether known. It was rich beyond a doubt, but they could learn only by trial what sort of seed suited it best. So they let that wait a while, and continued the work of making themselves tight and warm for the winter.

The skins of deer and buffalo and beaver, slain by the hunters, were dried in the sun, and they hung some of the finer ones on the walls of the rooms to make them look more cozy and picturesque. Mrs. Ware also put two or three on the floors, though the border women generally scorned them for such uses, thinking them in the way. Henry also helped his father make stools and chairs, the former a very simple task, consisting of a flat piece of wood, chopped or sawed out, in which three holes were bored to receive the legs, the latter made of a section of sapling, an inch or so in diameter. But the baskets required longer and more tedious work. They cut green withes, split them into strips and then plaiting them together formed the basket. In this Mrs. Ware and even the little girl helped. They also made tables and a small stone furnace or bake-oven for the kitchen.

Their chief room now looked very cozy. In one corner stood a bedstead with low, square posts, the bed covered with a pure white counterpane. At the foot of the bedstead was a large heavy chest, which served as bureau, sofa and dressing case. In the center of the room stood a big walnut table, on the top of which rested a nest of wooden trays, flanked, on one side, by a nicely folded tablecloth, and on the other by a butcher knife and a Bible. In a corner was a cupboard consisting of a set of shelves set into the logs, and on these shelves were the blue-edged plates and yellow-figured teacups and blue teapot that Mrs. Ware had received long ago from her mother. The furniture in the remainder of the house followed this pattern.

The heaviest labor of all was to extend the "clearing"; that is, to cut down trees and get the ground ready for planting the crops next spring, and in this Henry helped, for he was able to wield an ax blow for blow with a grown man. When he did not have to work he went often to the river, which was within sight of Wareville, and caught fish. Nobody except the men, who were always armed, and who knew how to take care of themselves, was allowed to go more than a mile from the palisade, but Henry was trusted as far as the river; then the watchman in the lookout on top of the highest blockhouse could see him or any who might come, and there, too, he often lingered.

He did not hate his work, yet he could not say that he liked it, and, although he did not know it, the love of the wild man's ways was creeping into his blood. The influence of the great forests, of the vast unknown spaces, was upon him. He could lie peacefully in the shade of a tree for an hour at a time, dreaming of rivers and mountains farther on in the depths of the wilderness. He felt a kinship with the wild things, and once as he lay perfectly still with his eyes almost closed, a stag, perhaps the brother to the one that he had killed, came and looked at him out of great soft eyes. It did not seem odd at the time to Henry that the stag should do so; he took it then as a friendly act, and lest he should alarm this new comrade of the woods he did not stir or even raise his eyelids. The stag gazed at him a few moments, and then, tossing his great antlers, turned and walked off in a graceful and dignified way through the woods. Henry wondered where the deer would go, and if it would be far. He wished that he, too, could roam the wilderness so lightly, wandering where he wished, having no cares and beholding new scenes every day. That would be a life worth living.

The next morning his mother said to his father:

"John, the boy is growing wild."

"Yes," replied the father. "They say it often happens with those who are taken young into the wilderness. The forest lays a spell upon them when they are easy to receive impressions."

The mother looked troubled, but Mr. Ware laughed.

"Don't bother about it," he said. "It can be cured. We have merely to teach him the sense of responsibility."

This they proceeded to do.

CHAPTER III
LOST IN THE WILDERNESS

THE method by which Mr. and Mrs. Ware undertook to teach Henry a sense of responsibility was an increase of work. Founding a new state was no light matter, and he must do his share. Since he loved to fish, it became his duty to supply the table with fish, and that, too, at regular hours, and he also began to think of traps and snares, which he would set in the autumn for game. It was always wise for the pioneer to save his powder and lead, the most valuable of his possessions and the hardest to obtain. Any food that could be procured without its use was a welcome addition.

But fishing remained his easiest task, and he did it all with a pole that he cut with his clasp knife, a string and a little piece of bent and stiffened wire. He caught perch, bass, suckers, trout, sunfish, catfish, and other kinds, the names of which he did not know. Sometimes when his hook and line had brought him all that was needed, and the day was hot, he would take off his clothing and plunge into the deep, cool pools. Often his friend, Paul Cotter, was with him. Paul was a year younger than Henry, and not so big. Hence the larger boy felt himself, in a certain sense, Paul's teacher and protector, which gave him a comfortable feeling, and a desire to help his comrade as much as he could.

He taught the smaller lad new tricks in swimming, and scarcely a day passed when two sunburned, barefooted boys did not go to the river, quickly throw off their clothing, and jump into the clear water. There they swam and floated for a long time, dived, and ducked each other, and then lay on the grass in the sun until they dried.

"Paul," said Henry once, as they were stretched thus on the bank, "wouldn't you like to have nothing to do, but wander through the woods just as you pleased, sleep wherever you wished, and kill game when you grew hungry, just like the Indians?"

Henry's eyes were on the black line of the forest, and the blue haze of the sky beyond. His spirit was away in the depths of the unknown.

"I don't know," replied Paul. "I guess a white boy has to become a white man, after a while, and they say that the difference between a white man and the Indian is that the white man has to work."

"But the Indians get along without it," said Henry.

"No they don't," replied Paul. "We win all the country because we've learned how to do things while we are working."

Yet Henry was unconvinced, and his thoughts wandered far into the black forest and the blue haze.

The cattle pastured near the deepest of the swimming holes, and it often fell to the lot of the boys to bring them into the palisade at sunset. This was a duty of no little importance, because if any of the cattle wandered away into the forest and were lost, they could not be replaced. It was now the latter half of summer, and the grass and foliage were fast turning brown in the heat. Late on the afternoon of one of the very hottest days Henry and Paul went to the deepest swimming hole. There had not been a breath of air stirring since morning; not a blade of grass, not a leaf quivered. The skies burned like a sheet of copper.

The boys panted, and their clothing, wet with perspiration, clung to them. The earth was hot under their feet. Quickly they threw off their

garments and sprang into the water. How cool and grateful it felt! There
they lingered long, and did not notice the sudden obscurity of the sun
and darkening of the southwest.

A slight wind sprang up presently, and the dry leaves and grass began to rustle. There was thunder in the distance and a stroke of lightning. The boys were aroused, and scrambling out of the water put on
their clothing.

"A storm's coming," said Henry, who was weatherwise, "and we
must get the cattle in."

These sons of the forest did not fear rain, but they hurried on their
clothing, and they noticed, too, how rapidly the storm was gathering.
The heat had been great for days, and the earth was parched and thirsty.
The men had talked in the evening of rain, and said how welcome it
would be, and now the boys shared the general feeling. The drought
would be ended. The thirsty earth would drink deep and grow green
again.

The rolling clouds, drawn like a great curtain over the southwest,
advanced and covered all the heavens. The flashes of lightning followed
each other so fast that, at times, they seemed continuous; the forest
groaned as it bent before the wind. Then the great drops fell, and soon
they were beating the earth like volleys of pistol bullets. Fragments of
boughs, stripped off by the wind, swept by. Never had the boys in their
Eastern home known such thunder and lightning. The roar of one was
always in their ears, and the flash of the other always in their eyes.

The frightened cattle were gathered into a group, pressing close together for company and protection. The boys hurried them toward the
stockade, but one cow, driven by terror, broke from the rest and ran
toward the woods. Agile Henry, not willing to lose a single straggler,
pursued the fugitive, and Paul, wishing to be as zealous, followed. The

rest of the cattle, being so near and obeying the force of habit, went on into the stockade.

It was the wildest cow of the herd that made a plunge for the woods, and Henry, knowing her nature, expected trouble. So he ran as fast as he could, and he was not aware until they were in the forest that Paul was close behind him. Then he shouted:

"Go back, Paul! I'll bring her in."

But Paul would not turn. There was fire in his blood. He considered it as much his duty to help as it was Henry's. Moreover, he would not desert his comrade.

The fugitive, driven by the storm acting upon its wild nature, continued at great speed, and the panting boys were not able to overtake her. So on the trio went, plunging through the woods, and saving themselves from falls, or collisions with trees, only by the light from the flashes of lightning. Many boys, even on the border, would have turned back, but there was something tenacious in Henry's nature; he had undertaken to do a thing, and he did not wish to give it up. Besides that cow was too valuable. And Paul would not leave his comrade.

Away the cow went, and behind her ran her pursuers. The rain came rushing and roaring through the woods, falling now in sheets, while overhead the lightning still burned, and the thunder still crashed, though with less frequency. Both the boys were drenched, but they did not mind it; they did not even know it at the time. The lightning died presently, the thunder ceased to rumble, and then the darkness fell like a great blanket over the whole forest. The chase was blotted out from them, and the two boys, stopping, grasped each other's hands for the sake of company. They could not see twenty feet before them, but the rain still poured.

"We'll have to give her up," said Henry reluctantly. "We couldn't follow a whole herd of buffaloes in all this black night."

"Maybe we can find her to-morrow," said Paul.

"Maybe so," replied Henry. "We've got to wait anyhow. Let's go home."

They started back for Wareville, keeping close together, lest they lose each other in the darkness, and they realized suddenly that they were uncomfortable. The rain was coming in such sheets directly in their faces that it half blinded them, now and then their feet sank deep in mire and their drenched bodies began to grow cold. The little log houses in which they lived now seemed to them palaces, fit for a king, and they hastened their footsteps, often tripping on vines or running into bushes. But Henry was trying to see through the dark woods.

"We ought to be near the clearing," he said.

They stopped and looked all about, seeking to see a light. They knew that one would be shining from the tower of the blockhouse as a guide to them. But they saw none. They had misjudged the distance, so they thought, and they pushed on a half hour longer, but there was still no light, nor did they come to a clearing. Then they paused. Dark as it was each saw a look of dismay on the face of the other.

"We've come the wrong way!" exclaimed Paul.

"Maybe we have," reluctantly admitted Henry.

But their dismay lasted only a little while. They were strong boys, used to the wilderness, and they did not fear even darkness and wandering through the woods. Moreover, they were sure that they should find Wareville long before midnight.

They changed their course and continued the search. The rain ceased by and by, the clouds left the heavens, and the moon came out, but they saw nothing familiar about them. The great woods were dripping with water, and it was the only sound they heard, besides that made by themselves. They stopped again, worn out and disconsolate at last. All their walking only served to confuse them the more. Neither now had any idea of the direction in which Wareville lay, and to be lost in the wilderness was a most desperate matter. They might travel a thousand miles, should strength last them for so great a journey, and never see a single human being. They leaned against the rough bark of a great oak tree, and stared blankly at each other.

"What are we to do?" asked Paul.

"I can't say," replied Henry.

The two boys still looked blank, but at last they laughed--and each laughed at the other's grewsome face. Then they began once more to cast about them. The cold had passed and warm winds were blowing up from the south. The forest was drying, and Henry and Paul, taking off their coats, wrung the water from them. They were strong lads, inured to many hardships of the border and the forest, and they did not fear ill results from a mere wetting. Nevertheless, they wished to be comfortable, and under the influence of the warm wind they soon found themselves dry again. But they were so intensely sleepy that they could scarcely keep their eyes open, and now the wilderness training of both came into use.

It was a hilly country, with many outcroppings of stone and cavelike openings in the sides of the steep but low hills, and such a place as this the boys now sought. But it was a long hunt and they grew more tired and sleepy at every step. They were hungry, too, but if they might only sleep they could forget that. They heard again the hooting of owls and the wind, moaning among the leaves, made strange noises. Once there was a crash in a thicket beside them, and they jumped in momentary alarm, but it was only a startled deer, far more scared than they, running through the bushes, and Henry was ashamed of his nervous impulse.

They found at last their resting place, a sheltered ledge of dry stone in the hollow of a hill. The stone arched above them, and it was dark in the recess, but the boys were too tired now to worry about shadows. They crept into the hollow, and, scraping up fallen leaves to soften the hard stone, lay down. Both were off to slumberland in less than five minutes.

The hollow faced the East, and the bright sun, shining into their eyes, awakened them at last. Henry sprang up, amazed. The skies were a silky blue, with little white clouds sailing here and there. The forest, new-washed by the rain, smelt clean and sweet. The south wind was still blowing. The world was bright and beautiful, but he was conscious of an acute pain at the center of his being. That is, he was increasingly hungry. Paul showed equal surprise, and was a prey to the same annoying sensation in an important region. He looked up at the sun, and found that it was almost directly overhead, indicating noon.

All the country about them was strange, an unbroken expanse of hill and forest, and nowhere a sign of a human being. They scrutinized the horizon with the keen eyes of boyhood, but they saw no line of smoke, rising from the chimneys of Wareville. Whether the villages lay north or south or east or west of them they did not know, and the wind that sighed so gently through the forest never told. They were alone in the wilderness and they knew, moreover, that the wilderness was very vast and they were very small. But Henry and Paul did not despair; in fact no such thought entered Henry's mind. Instead he began to find a certain joy in the situation; it appealed to his courage. They resolved to find something to eat, and they used first a temporary cure for the pangs of hunger. Each had a strong clasp knife and they cut strips of the soft inner bark of the slippery-elm tree, which they chewed, drawing from it a little strength and sustenance. They found an hour or two later some nearly ripe wild plums, which they ate in small quantities, and, later on, ripe blackberries very juicy and sweet. Paul wanted to be voracious, but Henry restrained him, knowing well that if he indulged liberally he might suffer worse pangs than those of hunger. Slender as was this diet the boys felt much strengthened, and their spirits rose in a wonderful manner.

"We're bound to be found sooner or later," said Henry, "and it's strange if we can't live in the woods until then."

"If we only had our guns and ammunition," said Paul, "we could get all the meat we wanted, and live as well as if we were at home."

This was true, because in the untrodden forest the game was plentiful all about them, but guns and ammunition they did not have, and it was vain to wish for them. They must obtain more solid food than wild plums and blackberries, if they would retain their strength, and both boys knew it. Yet they saw no way and they continued wandering until they came to a creek. They sat a while on its banks and looked down at the fish with which it was swarming, and which they could see distinctly in its clear waters.

"Oh, if we only had one of those fine fellows!" said Paul.

"Then why not have him?" exclaimed Henry, a sudden flash appearing in his eye.

"Yes, why not?" replied Paul with sarcasm. "I suppose that all we have to do is to whistle and the finest of 'em will come right out here on the bank, and ask us to cook and eat 'em."

"We haven't any hooks and lines now but we might make 'em," said Henry.

"Make 'em!" said Paul, and he looked in amazement at his comrade.

"Out of our clothes," replied Henry.

Then he proceeded to show what he meant and Paul, too, when he saw him begin, was quickly taken with the idea. They drew many long strands from the fiber of their clothing--cloth in those days was often made as strong as leather--and twisted and knotted them together until they had a line fifteen feet long. It took them at least two hours to complete this task, and then they contemplated their work with pride. But the look of joy on Paul's face did not last long.

"How on earth are we to get a hook, Henry?" he asked.

"I'll furnish that," replied Henry, and he took the small steel buckle with which his trousers were fastened together at the back. Breaking this apart he bent the slenderest portion of it into the shape of a hook, and fastened it to the end of his line.

"If we get a fish on this he may slip off or he may not, but we must try," he said.

The fishing rod and the bait were easy matters. A slender stem of dogwood, cut with a clasp knife, served for the first, and, to get the latter, they had nothing to do but turn up a flat stone, and draw angle worms from the moist earth beneath.

The hook was baited and with a triumphant flourish Henry swung it toward the stream.

"Now," he said, "for the biggest fish that ever swam in this creek."

The boys might have caught nothing with such a rude outfit, but doubtless that stream was never fished in before, and its inhabitants, besides being full of a natural curiosity, did not dream of any danger coming from the outer air. Therefore they bit at the curious-looking metallic thing with the tempting food upon it which was suddenly dropped from somewhere.

But the first fish slipped off as Henry had feared, and then there was nothing to do but try again. It was not until the sixth or seventh bite that he succeeded in landing a fine perch upon the bank, and then Paul uttered a cry of triumph, but Henry, as became his superior dignity at that moment, took his victory modestly. It was in reality something to rejoice over, as these two boys were perhaps in a more dangerous situation than they, with all their knowledge of the border, understood. The wilderness was full of animal life, but it was fleeter than man, and, without weapons they were helpless.

"And now to cook him," said Henry. So speaking, he took from his pocket the flint and steel that he had learned from the men always to carry, while Paul began to gather fallen brushwood.

To light the fire Henry expected to be the easiest of their tasks, but it proved to be one of the most difficult. He struck forth the elusive sparks again and again, but they went out before setting fire to the wood. He worked until his fingers ached and then Paul relieved him. It fell to the younger boy's lot to succeed. A bright spark flying forth rested a moment among the lightest and dryest of the twigs, igniting there. A tiny point of flame appeared, then grew and leaped up. In a few moments the great pile of brushwood was in a roaring blaze, and then the boys cooked their fish over the coals. They ate it all with supreme content, and they believed they could feel the blood flowing in a new current through their veins and their strength growing, too.

But they knew that they would have to prepare for the future and draw upon all their resources of mind and body. Their hook and line was but a slender appliance and they might not have such luck with it again. Paul suggested that they make a fish trap, of sticks tied together with strips cut from their clothing, and put it in the creek, and Henry thought it was a good idea, too. So they agreed to try it on the morrow, if they should not be found meanwhile, and then they debated the subject of snares.

The undergrowth was swarming with rabbits, and they would make most toothsome food. Rabbits they must have, and again Henry led the way. He selected a small clear spot near the thick undergrowth where a rabbit would naturally love to make his nest and around a circle about six inches in diameter he drove a number of smooth pegs. Then he tied a strong cord made of strips of their clothing to one end of a stout bush, which he bent over until it curved in a semicircle. The other end of the cord was drawn in a sliding loop around the pegs, and was attached to a little wooden trigger, set in the center of the inclosure.

The slightest pressure upon this trigger would upset it, cause the noose to slip off the pegs and close with a jerk around the neck of anything that might have its head thrust into the inclosure. The bush, too, would fly back into place and there would be the intruder, really hanged by himself. It was the common form of snare, devised for small game by the boys of early Kentucky, and still used by them.

Henry and Paul made four of these ingenious little contrivances, and baited them with bruised pieces of the small plantain leaves that the rabbits love. Then they contemplated their work again with satisfaction. But Paul suddenly began to look rueful.

"If we have to pay out part of our clothes every time we get a dinner we soon won't have any left," he said.

Henry only laughed.

It was now near sunset, and, as they had worked hard they would have been thankful for supper, but there was none to be thankful for, and they were too tired to fish again. So they concluded to go to sleep, which their hard work made very easy, and dream of abundant harvests on the morrow.

They gathered great armfuls of the fallen brushwood, littering the forest, and built a heap as high as their heads, which blazed and roared in a splendid manner, sending up, too, a column of smoke that rose far above the trees and trailed off in the blue sky.

It was a most cheerful bonfire, and it was a happy thought for the boys to build it, even aside from its uses as a signal, as the coming of night in the wilderness is always most lonesome and weird.

They lay down near each other on the soft turf, and Henry watched the red sun sink behind the black forest in the west. The strange, sympathetic feeling for the wilderness again came into his mind. He thought once more of the mysterious regions that lay beyond the line where the black and red met. He could live in the woods, he was living now without arms, even, and if he only had his rifle and ammunition he could live in luxury. And then the wonderful freedom! That old thought came to him with renewed force. To roam as he pleased, to stop when he pleased and to sleep where he pleased! He would make a canoe, and float down the great rivers to their mouths. Then he would wander far out on the vast plains, which they say lay beyond the thousand miles of forest, and see the buffalo in millions go thundering by. That would be a life without care.

He fell asleep presently, but he was awakened after a while by a long-drawn plaintive shriek answered by a similar cry. Once he would have been alarmed by the sound, but now he knew it was panther talking to panther. He and Paul were unarmed, but they had something as effective as guns against panthers and that was the great bonfire which still roared and blazed near them. He was glad now for a new reason that they had built it high, because the panther's cry was so uncanny and sent such a chill down one's back. He looked at Paul, but his comrade still slept soundly, a peaceful smile showing on his face. He remembered the words of Ross that no wild animal would trouble man if man did not trouble him, and, rolling a little nearer to Paul, he shut his eyes and sought sleep.

But sleep would not come, and presently he heard the cry of the panther again but much nearer. He was lying with his ear to the ground. Now the earth is a conductor of sound and Henry was sure that he heard a soft tread. He rose upon his elbow and gazed into the darkness. There he beheld at last a dim form moving with sinuous motion, and slowly it took the shape of a great cat-like animal. Then he saw just behind it another as large, and he knew that they were the two panthers whose cries he had heard.

Henry was not frightened, although there was something weird and uncanny in the spectacle of these two powerful beasts of prey, stealing about the fire, before which two unarmed boys reposed. He knew, however, that they were drawn not by the desire to attack, but by a kind of terrified curiosity. The fire was to them the magnet that the snake is to the fascinated bird. He longed then for his gun, the faithful little rifle that was reposing on the hooks over his bed in his father's house. "I'd make you cry for something," he said to himself, looking at the largest of the panthers.

The animals lingered, glaring at the boys and the fire with great red eyes, and presently Henry, doing as he had done on a former occasion, picked up a blazing torch and, shouting, rushed at them.

The panthers sprang headlong through the undergrowth, in their eagerness to get away from the terrible flaming vision that was darting down upon them. Their flight was so quick that they disappeared in an instant and Henry knew they would not venture near the site of the fire again in a long time. He turned back and found Paul surprised and alarmed standing erect and rubbing his eyes.

"Why--why--what's the matter?" cried Paul.

"Oh, it's nothing," replied Henry.

Then he told about the panthers. Paul did not know as much as Henry concerning panthers and the affair got on his nerves. The lonely and vast grandeur of the wilderness did not have the attraction for him that it had for his comrade, and he wished again for the strong log walls and comfortable roofs of Wareville. But Henry reassured him. The testimony of the hunters about the timidity of wild beasts was unanimous and he need have no fears. So Paul went to sleep again, but Henry lingered as before.

He threw fresh fuel on the fire. Then he lay down again and gradually weary nature became the master of him. The woods grew dim, and faded away, the fire vanished and he was in slumberland.

When Henry awoke it was because some one was tugging at his shoulder. He knew now that the Indian warriors had come across the Ohio, and had seized him, and he sprang up ready to make a fierce resistance.

"Don't fight, Henry! It's me--Paul!" cried a boyish voice, and Henry letting his muscles relax rubbed the sleep out of his eyes. It was Paul sure enough standing beside him, and the sun again was high up in the heavens. The fire was still burning, though it had died down somewhat.

"Oh, my breakfast!" cried Henry as he felt a sudden pang.

"Come, let's see if we're going to have any," said Paul, and off they went to their snares. The first had not been touched, nor had the second. The bait was gone from the third, and the loop sprung, but there was nothing in it. The hearts of the boys sank and they thought again of wild plums and blackberries which were but a light diet. But when they came to the fourth snare their triumph was complete. A fat rabbit, caught in the loop, was hanging by the neck, beside the bush.

"It's lucky the forest is so full of game that some of it falls into our trap," said Henry.

They cooked the rabbit, and again they were so hungry that they ate it all. Then they improvised new fishing tackle and both boys began to fish. They knew that they must devote their whole time to this problem of food, and they decided, for the present, not to leave the creek. They were afraid to renew the search for Wareville, lest they wander deeper into the wilderness, and moreover lose the way to the creek which seemed to be the surest source of food. So they would stay a while where they were, and keep their fire burning high as a signal to searchers.

Either the fish had learned that the curiously shaped thing with the tempting bait upon it was dangerous, or they had gone to visit friends in distant parts of the creek, for, at least two hours passed, without either boy getting a bite. When the fish did lay hold it was usually to slip again from the rude hook, and it was at least another hour before they caught a fish. It was Paul who achieved the feat, and it repaid him for being asleep when the panthers came, a matter that had lain upon his mind somewhat.

They persisted in this work until Henry also made a catch and then they gathered more plums and berries. They dug up, too, the root of the Indian turnip, an herb that burnt the mouth like fire, but which Henry said they could use, after soaking it a long time in water. Then they discussed the matter of the fish trap which they thought they could make in a day's work. This would relieve them of much toil, but they deferred its beginning until the morrow, and used the rest of the day in making two more snares for rabbits.

Paul now suggested that they accumulate as much food as possible, cook it and putting it on their backs follow the creek to its mouth. He had no doubt that it emptied into the river that flowed by Wareville and then by following the stream, if his surmise was right, they could reach home again. It was a plausible theory and Henry agreed with him. Meanwhile they built their fire high again and lay down for another night's rest in the woods. The next day they devoted to the fish trap which was successfully completed, and put in the river, and then they took their places on the turf for the third night beside the camp fire.

The day, like its predecessor, had been close and hot. All traces of the great rain were gone. Forest and earth were again as dry as tinder. They refreshed themselves with a swim in the creek just before lying down to sleep, but they were soon panting with the heat. It seemed to hang in heavy clouds, and the forest shut out any fresh air that might be moving high up.

Despite the great heat the boys had built the fire as high as usual, because they knew that the search for them would never cease so long as there was a hope of success, and they thought that the signal should not be lacking. But now they moved away from it and into the shadow of the woods.

"If only the wind would blow!" said Henry.

"And I'd be willing to stand a rain like the one in which we got lost," said Paul.

But neither rain nor wind came, and after a while they fell asleep. Henry was awakened at an unknown hour of the night by a roaring in his ears, and at first he believed that Paul was about to have his storm. Then he was dazzled by a great rush of light in his eyes, and he sprang to his feet in sudden alarm.

"Up, Paul!" he cried, grasping his comrade by the shoulder. "The woods are on fire!"

Paul was on his feet in an instant, and the two were just in time.

Sparks flew in their faces and the flames twisting into pyramids and columns leaped from tree to tree with a sound like thunder as they came. Boughs, burnt through, fell to the ground with a crash. The sparks rose in millions.

The boys had slept in their clothes or rather what was left of them, and, grasping each other's hands, they ran at full speed toward the creek, with the great fire roaring and rushing after them. Henry looked back once but the sight terrified him and the sparks scorched his face. He knew that the conflagration had been set by their own bonfire, fanned by a rising wind as they slept, but it was no time to lament. The rush and sweep of the flames, feeding upon the dry forest and gathering strength as they came, was terrific. It was indeed like the thunder of a storm in the ears of the frightened boys, and they fairly skimmed over the ground in the effort to escape the red pursuer. They could feel its hot breath on their necks, while the smoke and the sparks flew over their heads. They dashed into the creek, and each dived down under the water which felt so cool and refreshing.

"Let's stay here," said Paul, who enjoyed the present.

"We can't think of such a thing," replied Henry. "This creek won't stop that fire half a minute!"

A fire in a sun-dried Western forest is a terrible thing. It rushes on at a gallop, roaring and crackling like the battle-front of an army, and destroying everything that lies before it. It leaves but blackened stumps and charred logs behind, and it stops only when there is no longer food for it to devour.

The boys sprang out of the creek and ran up the hill. Henry paused a moment at its crest, and looked back again. The aspect of the fire was more frightful than ever. The flames leaped higher than the tops of the tallest trees, and thrust out long red twining arms, like coiling serpents.

Beneath was the solid red bank of the conflagration, preceded by showers of ashes and smoke and sparks. The roar increased and was like that of many great guns in battle.

"Paul!" exclaimed Henry seizing his comrade's hand again. "We've got to run, as we've never run before! It's for our lives now!"

It was in good truth for their lives, and bending low their heads, the two boys, hand in hand, raced through the forest, with the ruthless pursuer thundering after them. Henry as he ran, glanced back once more and saw that the fire was gaining upon them. The serpents of flame were coming nearer and nearer and the sparks flew over their heads in greater showers. Paul was panting, and being the younger and smaller of the two his strength was now failing. Henry felt his comrade dragging upon his hand. If he freed himself from Paul's grasp he could run faster, but he remembered his silent resolve to take Paul back to his people. Even were it not for those others at Wareville he could never desert his friend at such a moment. So he pulled on Paul's hand to hasten his speed, and together the boys went on.

The two noticed presently that they were not alone in their flight, a circumstance that had escaped them in the first hurry and confusion. Deer and rabbits, too, flew before the hurricane of fire. The deer were in a panic of terror, and a great stag ran for a few moments beside the boys, not noticing them, or, in his fear of greater evil, having no fear of human beings who were involved in the same danger. Three or four buffaloes, too, presently joined the frightened herd of game, one, a great bull running with head down and blowing steam from his nostrils.

Paul suddenly sank to his knees and gasped:

"I can't go on! Let me stay here and you save yourself, Henry!"

Henry looked back at the great fiery wall that swept over the ground, roaring like a storm. It was very near now and the smoke almost blinded him. A boy with a spirit less stanch than his might well have fled in a panic, leaving his companion to his death. But the nearer the danger came the more resolute Henry grew. He saw, too, that he must sting Paul into renewed action.

"Get up!" he exclaimed, and he jerked the fainting boy to his feet. Then, snatching a stick, he struck Paul several smart blows on his back. Paul cried out with the sudden pain, and, stimulated by it into physical action, began to run with renewed speed.

"That's right, Paul!" cried Henry, dropping his stick and seizing his comrade again by the hand. "One more big try and we'll get away! Just over this hill here it's open ground, and the fire will have to stop!"

It was a guess, only made to encourage Paul, and Henry had small hope that it would come true, but when they reached the brow of the hill both uttered a shout of delight. There was no forest for perhaps a quarter of a mile beyond, and down the center of the open glittered a silver streak that meant running water.

Henry was so joyous that he cried out again.

"See, Paul! See!" he exclaimed. "Here's safety! Now we'll run!"

How they did run! The sight gave them new strength. They shot out of that terrible forest and across the short dry grass, burnt brown by late summer days, running for life toward the flowing water. They did not stop to notice the size of the stream, but plunged at once into its current.

Henry sank with a mighty splash, and went down, down, it seemed to him, a mile. Then his feet touched a hard, rocky bottom, and he shot back to the surface, spluttering and blowing the water out of eyes, mouth and nostrils. A brown head was bobbing beside him. He seized it by the hair, pulled it up, and disclosed the features of Paul, his comrade. Paul, too, began to splutter and at the same time to try to swim.

Splash!

A heavy body struck the water beside them with a thud too great for that of a man. It was the stag leaping also for safety and he began to swim about, looking at the boys with great pathetic eyes, as if he would ask them what he ought to do next for his life. Apparently his fear of mankind had passed for the moment. They were bound together by the community of danger.

Splash! Splash! Splash!

The water resounded like the beating of a bass drum. Three more deer, a buffalo, and any number of smaller game sprang into the stream, and remained there swimming or wading.

"Here, Paul! Here's a bar that we can stand on," said Henry who had found a footing. At the same time he grasped Paul by the wrist, and drew him to the bar. There they stood in the water to their necks, and watched the great fire as it divided at the little prairie, and swept around them, passing to left and right. It was a grim sight. All the heavens seemed ablaze, and the clouds of smoke were suffocating. Even there in the river the heat was most oppressive, and at times the faces of the boys were almost scorched. Then they would thrust their heads under the water, and keep them there as long as they could hold their breath, coming up again greatly refreshed. The wild game clustered near in common terror.

"It's a lucky thing for us the river and prairie are here," said Henry. "Another half mile and we'd have been ashes."

Paul was giving thanks under his breath, and watching the fire with awe-stricken eyes. It swept past them and rushed on, in a great red cloud, that ate all in its path and gave forth much noise.

It was now on the far side of the prairie, and soon began to grow smaller in the distance. Yet so great was the wall of fire that it was long in sight, dying at last in a red band under the horizon. Even then all the skies were still filled with drifting smoke and ashes.

The boys looked back at the path over which they had come, and although the joy of escape was still upon them it was with real grief that they beheld the stricken forest, lately so grand a sight. It was now but a desolate and blackened ruin. Here and there charred trunks stood like the chimneys of burned houses, and others lay upon the ground like fallen and smoking rafters. Scattered about were great beds of living coals, where the brush had been thickest, and smoke rose in columns from the burned grass and hot earth. It was all like some great temple destroyed by fire; and such it was, the grandest of all temples, the natural temple of the forest.

"We kindled that fire," said Paul.

"I guess we did," responded Henry, "but we didn't know our spark would grow into so great a blaze."

They swam to the bank and walked toward the remains of the forest. But the ground was still hot to their feet, and the smoke troubled them. Near the edge of the wood they found a deer still alive and with a broken leg, tripped in its panic-stricken flight or struck by a fallen tree. Henry approached cautiously and slew him with his clasp knife. He felt strong pity as the fallen animal looked at him with great mournful eyes, but they were two hungry boys, and they must have a food supply if they would live in the woods.

They cleaned and dressed the deer and found that the carcass was as much as they could carry. But with great toil they lifted it over the hot ground, and then across another little prairie, until they came to woods only partially burned. There they hung the body to the bough of a tree, out of the reach of beasts of prey.

Then they took thought for the future. Barring the deer which would last some time they would now have to begin all over again, but they resolved to spend the rest of the present day, there under the shade of the trees. They were too much exhausted with exertion and excitement to undertake any new risk just yet.

Paul was afflicted with a great longing for home that afternoon. The fire and their narrow escape were still on his nerves. His muscular fiber was not so enduring as that of Henry, and the wilderness did not make so keen an appeal to him. Their hardships were beginning to weigh upon him and he thought all the time of Wareville, and the comfortable little log houses and the certain and easy supplies of food. Henry knew what was on his comrade's mind but he did not upbraid him for weakness of spirit. He, too, had memories of Wareville, and he pitied the grief of their people who must now be mourning them as lost forever. But he had been thinking long and hard and he had a plan. Finally he announced to Paul that they would build a raft.

"I believe this is the same river that runs by Wareville," he said. "I never heard Ross or Shif'less Sol or any of the men speak of another river, near enough for us to have reached it, since we've been wandering around. So it must be the same. Now either we are above Wareville or we are below it. We've got to guess at that and take the risk of it. We can roll a lot of the logs and timber into the river, tie 'em together, and float with the stream until we come to Wareville."

"But if we never come to it?" asked Paul.

"Then all we have to do is to get off the raft and follow the river back up the bank. Then we are sure to reach home."

This was so plausible that Paul was full of enthusiasm and they decided that they would set to work on the raft early in the morning.

CHAPTER IV
THE HAUNTED FOREST

AS the two boys sat before their camp fire that night, after making their plan, they were far from feeling gloomy. Another revulsion had come. Safe, for the moment, after their recent run for life, it seemed to them that they were safe for all time. They were rested, they had eaten good food in plenty, and the fire was long since but a dim red blur on the horizon. Ashes, picked up by wandering puffs of wind, still floated here and there among the burned tree trunks, and now and then a shower of sparks burst forth, as a bough into which the flames had eaten deep, broke and fell to the ground; but fear had gone from the lads, and, in its place, came a deep content. They were used to the forest, and in the company of each other they felt neither loneliness nor despair.

"It's good here," said Paul who was a reader and a philosopher. "I guess a fellow's life looks best to him just after he's thought he was going to lose it, but didn't."

"I think that's true," said Henry, glancing toward the far horizon, where the red blur still showed under the twilight. "But that was just a little too close for fun."

But his satisfaction was even deeper than Paul's. The wilderness and its ways made a stronger appeal to him. Paul, without Henry, would have felt loneliness and fear, but Henry alone, would have faced the night undaunted. Already the great forest was putting upon him its magic spell.

"Have you eaten enough, Paul?" he asked.

"I should like to eat more, but I'm afraid I can't find a place for it," replied Paul ruefully.

Henry laughed. He felt himself more than ever Paul's protector and regarded all his weaknesses with kindly tolerance. There the two lay awhile, stretched out on the soft, warm earth, watching the twilight deepen into night. Henry was listening to the voice of the wilderness, which spoke to him in such pleasant tones. He heard a faint sighing, like some one lightly plucking the strings of a guitar, and he knew that it was the wandering breeze among the burned boughs; he heard now and then a distant thud, and he knew that it was the fall of a tree, into whose trunk the flames had bit deeply; as he lay with his ear to the earth he heard more than once a furtive footfall as light as air, and he knew that some wild animal was passing. But he had no fear, the fire was a ring of steel about them.

Paul heard few of these sounds, or if hearing them he paid no heed. The wilderness was not talking to him. He was merely in the woods and he was very glad indeed to have his strong and faithful comrade beside him.

The twilight slipped away and the night came, thick and dark. The red blur lingered, but the faintest line of pink under the dark horizon, and the scorched tree trunks that curved like columns in a circle around them became misty and unreal. Despite himself Paul began to feel a little fear. He was a brave boy, but this was the wilderness, the wilderness in the dark, peopled by wild animals and perhaps by wilder men, and they were lost in it. He moved a little closer to his comrade. But

Henry, into whose mind no such thoughts had come, rose presently, and heaped more wood on the fire. He was merely taking an ordinary precaution, and this little task finished, he spoke to Paul in a vein of humor, purposely making his words sound very big.

"Mr. Cotter," he said, "it seems to me that two worthy gentlemen like ourselves who have had a day of hard toil should retire for the night, and seek the rest that we deserve."

"What you say is certainly true, Mr. Ware," responded Paul who had a lively fancy, "and I am glad to see that we have happened upon an inn, worthy of our great merits, and of our high position in life. This, you see, Mr. Ware, is the Kaintuckee Inn, a most spacious place, noted for its pure air, and the great abundance of it. In truth, Mr. Ware, I may assert to you that the ventilation is perfect."

"So I see, Mr. Cotter," said Henry, pursuing the same humor. "It is indeed a noble place. We are not troubled by any guest, beneath us in quality, nor are we crowded by any of our fellow lodgers."

"True! True!" said Paul, his bright eyes shining with his quick spirit, "and it is a most noble apartment that we have chosen. I have seldom been in one more spacious. My eyes are good, but good as they are I cannot see the ceiling, it is so high. I look to right and left, and the walls are so far away that they are hidden in the dark."

"Correctly spoken, Mr. Cotter," said Henry taking up the thread of talk, "and our inn has more than size to speak for it. It is furnished most beautifully. I do not know of another that has in it so good a larder. Its great specialty is game. It has too a most wonderful and plenteous supply of pure fresh water and that being so I propose that we get a drink and go to bed."

The two boys went down to the little brook that ran near, and drank heartily. They then returned within the ring of fire.

They were thoroughly tired and sleepy, and they quickly threw themselves down upon the soft warm earth, pillowing their heads on their arms, and the great Kaintuckee Inn bent over them a roof of soft, summer skies.

But the wilderness never sleeps, and its people knew that night that a stranger breed was abroad among them. The wind rose a little, and its song among the burned branches became by turns a music and a moan. The last cinder died, the earth cooled, and the forest creatures began to stir in the woodland aisles where the fire had passed. The disaster had come and gone, and perhaps it was already out of their memories forever. Rabbits timidly sought their old nests. A wild cat climbed a tree, scarcely yet cool beneath his claws, and looked with red and staring eyes at the ring of fire that formed a core of light in the forest, and the two extraordinary beings that slept within its shelter. A deer came down to the brook to drink, snorted at the sight of the red gleam among the trees, and then, when the strange odor came on the wind to its nostrils, fled in wild fright through the forest.

The news, in some way unknown to man, was carried to all the forest creatures. A new species, strange, unexplainable, had come among them, and they were filled with curiosity. Even the weak who had need to fear the strong, edged as near as they dared, and gazed at the singular beings who lay inside the red blaze. The wild cat crawled far out on the bare bough, and stared, half afraid, half curious, and also angry at the intrusion. He could see over the red blaze and he saw the boys stretched upon the ground, their faces, very white to the eye of the forest, upturned to the sky. To human gaze they would have seemed as two dead, but the keen eyes of the wild cat saw their chests rising and falling with deep regular breaths.

The darkness deepened and then after a while began to lighten. A beautiful clear moon came out and sheathed all the burned forest in gleaming silver. But the boys were still far away in a happy slumberland. The wild cat fled in alarm at the light, and the timid things drew back farther among the trees.

Time passed, and the red ring of fire about Paul and Henry sank. Hasty and tired, they had not drawn up enough wood to last out the night, and now the flames died, one by one. Then the coals smoldered and after a while they too began to go out, one by one. The red ring of fire that inclosed the two boys was slowly going away. It broke into links, and then the links went out.

Light clouds came up from the west, and were drawn, like a veil, across the sky. The moon began to fade, the silver armor melted away from the trees, and the wild cat that had come back could scarcely see the two strange beings, keen though his eyes were, so dense was the shadow where they lay. The wild things, still devoured with curiosity, pressed nearer. The terrible red light that filled their souls with dread, was gone, and the forest had lost half its terror. There was a ring of eyes about Henry and Paul, but they yet abode in glorious slumberland, peaceful and happy.

Suddenly a new note came into the sounds of the wilderness, one that made the timid creatures tremble again with dread. It was faint and very far, more like a quaver brought down upon the wind, but the ring of eyes drew back into the forest, and then, when the quaver came a second time, the rabbits and the deer fled, not to return. The lips of the wild cat contracted into a snarl, but his courage was only of the moment, he scampered away and he did not stop until he had gone a full mile. Then he swiftly climbed the tallest tree that he could find, and hid in its top.

The ring of eyes was gone, as the ring of fire had died, but Henry and Paul slept on, although there was full need for them to be awake. The long, distant quaver, like a whine, but with something singularly ferocious in its note came again on the wind, and, far away, a score of forms, phantom and dusky, in the shadow were running fast, with low, slim bodies, and outstretched nostrils that had in them a grateful odor of food, soon to come.

Nature had given to Henry Ware a physical mechanism of great strength, but as delicate as that of a watch. Any jar to the wheels and springs was registered at once by the minute hand of his brain. He stirred in his sleep and moved one hand in a troubled way. He was not yet awake, but the minute hand was quivering, and through all his wonderfully sensitive organism ran the note of alarm. He stirred again and then abruptly sat up, his eyes wide open, and his whole frame tense with a new and terrible sensation. He saw the dead coals, where the fire had been; the long, quavering and ferocious whine came to his ears, and, in an instant, he understood. It was well for the two that Henry was by nature a creature of the forest! He sprang to his feet and with one sweeping motion pulled Paul to his also.

"Up! Up, Paul!" he cried. "The fire is out, and the wolves are coming!"

Paul's physical senses were less acute and delicate than Henry's, and he did not understand at once. He was still dazed, and groping with his hands in the dusk, but Henry gave him no time.

"It's our lives, Paul!" he cried. "Another enemy as bad as the fire is after us!"

Not twenty feet away grew a giant beech, spreading out low and mighty boughs, and Henry leaped for it, dragging Paul after him.

"Up you go!" he cried, and Paul, not yet fully awake, instinctively obeyed the fierce command. Then Henry leaped lightly after him and as they climbed higher among the boughs the ferocious whine burst into a long terrible howl, and the dusky forms, running low, gaunt and ghostly in the shadow, shot from the forest, and hurled themselves at the beech tree.

Henry, despite all his courage, shuddered, and while he clutched a bough tightly with one hand put the other upon his comrade to see that he did not fall. He could feel Paul trembling in his grasp.

The two looked down upon the inflamed red eyes, the cruelly sharp, white teeth and slavering mouths, and, still panting from their climb, each breathed a silent prayer of thankfulness. They had been just in time to escape a pack of wolves that howled horribly for a while, and then sat upon their haunches, staring silently up at the sweet new food, which they believed would fall at last into their mouths.

Paul at length said weakly:

"Henry, I'm mighty glad you're a light sleeper. If it had been left to me to wake up first I'd have woke up right in the middle of the stomachs of those wolves."

"Well, we're here and we're safe for the present," said Henry who never troubled himself over what was past and gone, "and I think this is a mighty fine beech tree. I know that you and I, Paul, will never see another so big and friendly and good as it is."

Paul laughed, now with more heart.

"You are right, Henry," he said. "You are a mighty good friend, Mr. Big Beech Tree, and as a mark of gratitude I shall kiss you right in the middle of your honest barky old forehead," and he touched his lips lightly to the great trunk. Paul was an imaginative boy, and his whim pleased him. Such a thought would not have come to Henry, but he liked it in Paul.

"I think it's past midnight, Paul," said Henry, "and we've been lucky enough to have had several hours' sleep."

"But they'll go away as soon as they realize they can't get us," said Paul, "and then we can climb down and build a new and bigger ring of fire about us."

Henry shook his head.

"They don't realize it," he replied. "I know they expect just the contrary, Paul. They are as sure as a wolf can be that we will drop right into their mouths, just ready and anxious to be eaten. Look at that old fellow with his forepaws on the tree! Did you ever see such confidence?"

Paul looked down fearfully, and the eyes of the biggest of the wolves met his, and held him as if he were charmed. The wolf began to whine and lick his lips, and Paul felt an insane desire to throw himself down.

"Stop it, Paul!" Henry cried sharply.

Paul jerked his eyes away, and shuddered from head to foot.

"He was asking me to come," he said hysterically, "and I don't know how it was, but for a moment I felt like going."

"Yes and a warm welcome he would have given you," said Henry still sharply. "Remember that your best friend just now is not Mr. Big Wolf, but Mr. Big Beech Tree, and it's a wise boy who sticks to his best friend."

"I'm not likely to forget it," said Paul.

He shuddered again at the memory of the terrible, haunting eyes that had been able for a brief moment to draw him downward. Then he clasped the friendly tree more tightly in his arms, and Henry smiled approval.

"That's right, Paul," he said, "hold fast. I'd a heap rather be up here than down there."

Paul felt himself with his hand.

"I'm all in one piece up here," he said, "and I think that's good for a fellow who wants to live and grow."

Henry laughed with genuine enjoyment. Paul was getting back his sense of humor, and the change meant that his comrade was once more strong and alert. Then the larger boy looked down at their besiegers, who were sitting in a solemn circle, gazing now at the two lads and now at the venison, hanging from the boughs of another tree very near. In the dusk and the shadows they were a terrible company, gaunt and ghostly, gray and grim.

For a long time the wolves neither moved nor uttered a sound; they merely sat on their haunches and stared upward at the living prey that they felt would surely be theirs. The clouds, caught by wandering breezes, were stripped from the face of the sky, and the moonlight came out again, clear, and full, sheathing the scorched trunks once more in silver armor, and stretching great blankets of light on the burned and ashy earth. It fell too on the gaunt figures of the gray wolves, but the silent and deadly circle did not stir. In the moonlight they grew more terrible, the red eyes became more inflamed and angry, because they had to wait so long for what they considered theirs by right, the snarling lips were drawn back a little farther, and the sharp white teeth gleamed more cruelly.

Time passed again, dragging slowly and heavily for the besieged boys in the tree, but the wolves, though hungry, were patient. Strong in union they were lords of the forest, and they felt no fear. A shambling black bear, lumbering through the woods, suddenly threw up his nose in the wind, and catching the strong pungent odor, wheeled abruptly, lumbering off on another course. The wild cat did not come back, but crouched lower in his tree top; the timid things remained hidden deep in their nests and burrows.

It was a new kind of game that the wolves had scented and driven to the boughs, something that they had never seen before, but the odor was very sweet and pleasant in their nostrils. It was a tidbit that they must have, and, red-eyed, they stared at the two strange, toothsome creatures, who stirred now and then in the tree, and who made queer sounds to each other. When they heard these occasional noises the pack would reply with a long ferocious whine that seemed to double on itself and give back echoes from every point of the compass. In the still night it went far, and the timid things, when they heard it, trembled all over in their nests and burrows. Then the leader, the largest and most terrible of the pack would stretch himself upon the tree trunk, and claw at the scorched bark, but the food he craved was still out of reach.

They noticed that the strange creatures in the tree began to move oftener, and to draw their limbs up as if they were growing stiff, and then their long-drawn howl grew longer and more ferocious than ever; the game, tired out, would soon drop into their mouths. But it did not, the two creatures made sounds as if they were again encouraging each other, and the hearts of the wolves filled with rage and impatience that they should be cheated so long.

The night advanced; the moonlight faded again and the dark hours that come before the dawn were at hand. The forest became black and misty like a haunted wood, and the dim forms of the wolves were the ghosts that lived in it. But to their sharp red eyes the dark was nothing; they saw the two beings in the tree do a very queer thing; they tore strips from themselves, so it seemed to the wolves, from their clothing in fact, and wound it about their bodies and a bough of the tree against which they rested. But the wolves did not understand, only they knew that the creatures did not stir again or make any kind of noise for a long time.

When the darkness was thickest the wolves grew hot with impatience. Already they smelled the dawn and in the light their courage would ooze. Could it be that the food they coveted would not fall into their mouths? The dread suspicion filled every vein of the old leader with wrath, and he uttered a long terrible howl of doubt and anger; the pack took up the note and the lonely forest became alive with its echoes. But the creatures in the tree stirred only a little, and made very few sounds. They seemed to be safe and content, and the wolves raged back and forth, leaping and howling.

The old leader felt the dark thin and lighten, and the scent of the coming dawn became more oppressive to him. A little needle of fear shot into his heart, and his muscles began to grow weak. He saw afar in the east the first pale tinge, faint and gray, of the dreadful light that he feared and hated. His howl now was one of mingled anger and disap-pointment, and the pack imitated the note of the king.

The black veil over the forest gave way to one of gray. The dreadful bar of light in the east broadened and deepened, and became beaming, intense and brilliant. The needle of terror at the heart of the gray wolf stabbed and tore. His red eyes could not face the great red sun that swung now above the earth, shooting its fierce beams straight at him. The dark, so kindly and so encouraging, beloved of his kind, was gone, and the earth swam in a hideous light, every ray of which was hostile. His blood changed to water, his knees bent under him, and then, to turn fear to panic, came a powerful odor on the light, morning wind. It was like the scent of the two strange, succulent creatures in the tree, but it was the odor of many--many make strength he knew--and the great gray wolf was sore afraid.

The sun shot higher and the world was bathed in a luminous golden glow. The master-wolf cast one last, longing look at the lost food in the tree, and then, uttering a long quavering howl of terror, which the pack took up and carried in many echoes, fled headlong through the forest with his followers close behind, all running low and fast, and with terror hot at their heels. Their gaunt, gray bodies were gone in a moment, like ghosts that vanish at the coming of the day.

"Rouse up, Paul!" cried Henry. "They are gone, afraid of the sun, and it's safe for us now on the ground."

"And mighty glad I am!" said Paul. "The great Inn of Kaintuckee was not so hospitable after all, or at least some of our fellow guests were too hungry."

"It's because we were careless about our fire," said Henry. "If we had obeyed all the rules of the inn, we should have had no trouble. Jump down, Paul!"

Henry dropped lightly and cheerfully to the ground. As usual he let the past and its dangers slip, forgotten, behind him. Paul alighted beside him and the wilderness witnessed the strange sight of two stout boys, running up and down, pounding and rubbing their hands and arms, uttering little cries of pain, as the blood flowed at first slowly and with difficulty in their cramped limbs, and then of delight, as the circulation became free and easy.

"Now for breakfast," said Henry. "It will be easy, as Mr. Landlord has kept the venison hanging on the tree there for us."

Henry was breathing the fresh morning air, and rejoicing in the sunlight. His wonderful physical nature had cast away all thought of fear, but Paul, who had the sensitive mind and delicate fancy, was still troubled.

"Henry," he said, "I'm not willing to stay here, even to eat the deer meat. All through those hours we were up there it was a haunted forest for me. I don't want to see this spot any more, and I'd like to get away from it just as soon as I can."

Was it some instinct? or an unseen warning given to Paul, and registered on his sensitive mind, as a photographic plate takes light? To the keen nose of the old wolf leader an alarming odor had come with the dawn! Was a kindred signal sent to Paul?

Henry stared at his comrade in surprise, but he knew that he and Paul were different, and he respected those differences which might be either strength or weakness.

"All right, if you wish it, Paul," he said, lightly. "There are many rooms in the Kaintuckee Inn, and if the one we have doesn't suit us we'll just take another. Wait till I cut this venison down, and we'll move without paying our score."

"I guess we paid that to the wolves," said Paul, smiling a little.

Henry detached the venison and divided it. Then each took his share, and they moved swiftly away among the trees, still keeping to the general course of the river. They came presently to a large area of unburned forest, thick with foliage and undergrowth and, without hesitation, they plunged into it. Henry was in front and suddenly to his keen ears came a sound which he knew was not one of the natural noises of the forest. He listened and it continued, a beat, faint but regular and steady. He knew that it was made by footfalls, and he knew, too, that in the wilderness everyone is an enemy until he is proved to be a friend. They were in the densest of the undergrowth, and thought and action came to him on the heels of each other, swift as lightning.

"Sink down, Paul! Sink down!" he cried, and grasping his comrade by the shoulder he bore him down among the thick bushes, going down with him.

"Don't move for your life!" he whispered. "Men are about to pass and they cannot be our kind!"

Paul at once became as still as death. He too under the strain of the wilderness life and the need of caring for oneself was becoming wonderfully acute of the senses and ready of action. The two boys crouched close together, their heads below the tops of the bushes, although they could see between the leaves and twigs, and neither moved a hair.

Almost hidden in the foliage a line of Indian warriors, like dusky phantoms, passed, in single file, and apparently stepping in one another's tracks. Well for the boys that Paul had felt his impulse to leave the vicinity of the besieged tree, because the course of the warriors would carry them very near it, and they could not fail to detect the alien presence. But no such suspicion seemed to enter their minds now, and, like the wolves, they were traveling fast, but southward.

The boys stared through the leaves and twigs, afraid but fascinated. They were fourteen in all--Henry counted them--but never a warrior spoke a word, and the grim line was seen but a moment and then gone, though their dark painted faces long remained engraved, like pictures, on the minds of both. But to Paul it was, for the instant, like a dream. He saw them, and then he did not. The leaves of the bushes rustled a little when they passed, and then were still.

"They must be Southern Indians," whispered Henry. "Cherokees most likely. They come up here now and then to hunt, but they seldom stay long, for fear of the more warlike and powerful Northern Indians, who come down to Kaintuckee for the same purpose, at least that's what I heard Ross and Sol say."

"Well, they did seem to be traveling fast," breathed Paul, "and I'm mighty glad of it. Do you think, Henry, they could have done any harm at Wareville?"

Henry shook his head.

"I have no such fear," he said. "We are a good long distance from home, and they've probably gone by without ever hearing of the place.

Ross has always said that no danger was to be dreaded from the south."

"I guess it's so," said Paul with deep relief, "but I think, Henry, that you and I ought to go down to the river's bank, and build that raft as soon as we can."

"All right," said Henry calmly. "But we'll first eat our venison."

They quickly did as they agreed, and felt greatly strengthened and encouraged after a hearty breakfast. Then with bold hearts and quick hands they began their task.

CHAPTER V
AFLOAT

THE boys began at once the work on their raft, a rude structure of a few fallen logs, fastened together with bark and brush, but simple, strong and safe. They finished it in two days, existing meanwhile on the deer meat, and early the morning afterwards, the clumsy craft, bearing the two navigators, was duly intrusted to the mercy of the unknown river. Each of the boys carried a slender hickory pole with which to steer, and they also fastened securely to the raft the remainder of their deer, their most precious possession.

They pushed off with the poles, and the current catching their craft, carried it gently along. It was a fine little river, running in a deep channel, and Henry became more sure than ever that it was the one that flowed by Wareville. He was certain that the family resemblance was too strong for him to be mistaken.

They floated on for hours, rarely using their poles to increase the speed of the raft and by and by they began to pass between cliffs of considerable height. The forest here was very dense. Mighty oaks and hickories grew right at the water's edge, throwing out their boughs so far that often the whole stream was in the shade. Henry enjoyed it. This was one of the things that his fancy had pictured. He was now floating down an unknown river, through unknown lands, and, like as not, his and Paul's were the first human eyes that had ever looked upon these hills and splendid forests. Reposing now after work and danger he breathed again the breath of the wilderness. He loved it--its silence, its magnificent spaces, and its majesty. He was glad that he had come to Kentucky, where life was so much grander than it was back in the old Eastern regions. Here one was not fenced in and confined and could grow to his true stature.

They ate their dinner on the raft, still floating peacefully and tried to guess how far they had come, but neither was able to judge the speed of the current. Paul fitted himself into a snug place on their queer craft and after a while went to sleep. Henry watched him, lest he turn over and fall into the river and also kept an eye out for other things.

He was watching thus, when about the middle of the afternoon he saw a thin dark line, lying like a thread, against the blue skies. He studied it long and came to the conclusion that it was smoke.

"Smoke!" said he to himself. "Maybe that means Wareville."

The raft glided gently with the current, moving so smoothly and peacefully that it was like the floating of a bubble on a summer sea. Paul still lay in a dreamless sleep. The water was silver in the shade and dim gold where the sunshine fell upon it, and the trees, a solid mass, touched already by the brown of early autumn, dropped over the stream. Afar, a fine haze, like a misty veil, hung over the forest. The world was full of peace and primitive beauty.

They drifted on and the spire of smoke broadened and grew. The look of the river became more and more familiar. Paul still slept and Henry would not awaken him. He looked at the face of his comrade as he slumbered and noticed for the first time that it was thin and pale. The life in the woods had been hard upon Paul. Henry did not realize until this moment how very hard it had been. The sight of that smoke had not come too soon.

There was a shout from the bank followed by the crash of bodies among the undergrowth.

"Smoke me, but here they are! A-floatin' down the river in their own boat, as comfortable as two lords!"

It was the voice of Shif'less Sol, and his face, side by side with that of Ross, the guide, appeared among the trees at the river's brink. Henry felt a great flush of joy when he saw them, and waved his hands. Paul, awakened by the shouts, was in a daze at first, but when he beheld old friends again his delight was intense.

Henry thrust a pole against the bottom and shoved the raft to the bank. Then he and Paul sprang ashore and shook hands again and again with Ross and Sol. Ross told of the long search for the two boys. He and Mr. Ware and Shif'less Sol and a half dozen others had never ceased to seek them. They feared at one time that they had been carried off by savages, but nowhere did they find Indian traces. Then their dread was of starvation or death by wild animals, and they had begun to lose hope.

Both Henry and Paul were deeply moved by the story of the grief at Wareville. They knew even without the telling that this sorrow had never been demonstrative. The mothers of the West were too much accustomed to great tragedies to cry out and wring their hands when a blow fell. Theirs was always a silent grief, but none the less deep.

Then, guided by Ross and the shiftless one, they proceeded to Wareville which was really at the bottom of the smoke spire, where they were received, as two risen from the dead, in a welcome that was not noisy, but deep and heartfelt. The cow, the original cause of the trouble, had wandered back home long ago.

"How did you live in the forest?" asked Mr. Ware of Henry, after the first joy of welcome was shown.

"It was hard at first, but we were beginning to learn," replied the boy. "If we'd only had our rifles 'twould have been no trouble. And father, the wilderness is splendid!"

The boy's thoughts wandered far away for a moment to the wild woods where he again lay in the shade of mighty oaks and saw the deer come down to drink. Mr. Ware noticed the expression on Henry's face and took reflection. "I must not let the yoke bear too heavy upon him," was his unspoken thought.

But Paul's joy was unalloyed; he preferred life at Wareville to life in the wilderness amid perpetual hardships, and when they gave the great dinner at Mr. Ware's to celebrate the return of the wanderers he reached the height of human bliss. Both Ross and Shif'less Sol were present and with them, too, were Silas Pennypacker who could preach upon occasion for the settlement and did it, now and then, and John Upton, who next to Mr. Ware was the most notable man in Wareville, and his daughter Lucy, now a shy, pretty girl of twelve, and more than twenty others. Even Braxton Wyatt was among the members although he still sneered at Henry.

Theirs was in very truth a table fit for a king. In fact few kings could duplicate it, without sending to the uttermost parts of the earth, and perhaps not then. Meat was its staple. They had wild duck, wild goose, wild turkey, deer, elk, beaver tail, and a half dozen kinds of fish; but the great delicacy was buffalo hump cooked in a peculiar way--that is, served up in the hide of a buffalo from which the hair had been singed off, and baked in an earthen oven. Ross, who had learned it from the Indians, showed them how to do this, and they agreed that none of them had ever before tasted so fine a dish. When the dinner was over, Henry and Paul had to answer many questions about their wanderings, and they were quite willing to do so, feeling at the moment a due sense of their own importance.

A shade passed over the faces of some of the men at the mention of the Indians, whom Henry and Paul had seen, but Ross agreed with Henry that they were surely of the South, going home from a hunting trip, and so they were soon forgotten.

Henry's work after their return included an occasional hunting excursion, as game was always needed. His love of the wilderness did not decrease when thus he ranged through it and began to understand its ways. Familiarity did not breed contempt. The magnificent spaces and mighty silence appealed to him with increasing force. The columns of the trees were like cathedral aisles and the pure breath of the wind was fresh with life.

The first part of the autumn was hot and dry. The foliage died fast, the leaves twisted and dried up and the brown grass stems fell lifeless to the earth. A long time they were without rain, and a dull haze of heat hung over the simmering earth. The river shrank in its bed, and the brooks became rills.

Henry still hunted with his older comrades, though often at night now, and he saw the forest in a new phase. Dried and burned it appealed to him still. He learned to sleep lightly, that is, to start up at the slightest sound, and one morning after the wilderness had been growing hotter and dryer than ever he was awakened by a faint liquid touch on the roof. He knew at once that it was the rain, wished for so long and talked of so much, and he opened the shutter window to see it fall.

The sun was just rising, but showed only a faint glow of pink through the misty clouds, and the wind was light. The clouds opened but a little at first and the great drops fell slowly. The hot earth steamed at the touch, and, burning with thirst, quickly drank in the moisture. The wind grew and the drops fell faster. The heat fled away, driven by the waves of cool, fresh air that came out of the west. Washed by the rain the dry grass straightened up, and the dying leaves opened out, springing into new life. Faster and faster came the drops and now the sound they made was like the steady patter of musketry. Henry opened his mouth and breathed the fresh clean air, and he felt that like the leaves and grass he, too, was gaining new life.

When he went forth the next day in the dripping forest the wilderness seemed to be alive. The game swarmed everywhere and he was a lazy man who could not take what he wished. It was like a late touch of spring, but it did not last long, for then the frosts came, the air grew crisp and cool and the foliage of the forest turned to wonderful reds and yellows and browns. From the summit of the blockhouse tower Henry saw a great blaze of varied color, and he thought that he liked this part of the year best. He could feel his own strength grow, and now that cold weather was soon to come he would learn new ways to seek game and new phases of the wilderness.

The autumn and its beauty deepened. The colors of the foliage grew more intense and burned afar like flame. The settlers lightened their work and most of them now spent a large part of the time in hunting, pursuing it with the keen zest, born of a natural taste and the relaxation from heavy labors. Mr. Ware and a few others, anxious to test the qualities of the soil, were plowing up newly cleared land to be sown in wheat, but Henry was compelled to devote only a portion of his time to this work. The remaining hours, not needed for sleep, he was usually in the forest with Paul and the others.

The hunting was now glorious. Less than three miles from the fort and about a mile from the river Henry and Paul found a beaver dam across a tributary creek and they laid rude traps for its builders, six of which they caught in the course of time. Ross and Sol showed them how to take off the pelts which would be of value when trade should be opened with the east, and also how to cook beaver tail, a dish which could, with truth, be called a rival of buffalo hump.

Now the settlers began to accumulate a great supply of game at Wareville. Elk and deer and bear and buffalo and smaller animals were being jerked and dried at every house, and every larder was filled to the brim. There could be no lack of food the coming winter, the settlers said, and they spoke with some pride of their care and providence.

The village was gaining in both comfort and picturesqueness. Tanned skins of the deer, elk, buffalo, bear, wolf, panther and wild cat hung on the walls of every house, and were spread on every floor. The women contrived fans and ornaments of the beautiful mottled plumage of the wild turkey. Cloth was hard to obtain in the wilderness, as it might be a year before a pack train would come over the mountains from the east, and so the women made clothing of the softest and lightest of the dressed deer skin. There were hunting shirts for the men and boys, fastened at the waist by a belt, and with a fringe three or four inches long, the bottom of which fell to the knees. The men and boys also made themselves caps of raccoon skin with the tail sewed on behind as a decoration. Henry and Paul were very proud of theirs.

The finest robes of buffalo skin were saved for the beds, and Ross gave warning that they should have full need of them. Winters in Kentucky, he said, were often cold enough to freeze the very marrow in one's bones, when even the wildest of men would be glad enough to leave the woods and hover over a big fire. But the settlers provided for this also by building great stacks of firewood beside each house. They were as well equipped with axes--keen, heavy weapons--as they were with rifles and ammunition, and these were as necessary. The forest around Wareville already gave great proof of their prowess with the ax.

Now the autumn was waning. Every morning the wilderness gleamed and sparkled beneath a beautiful covering of white frost. The brown in the leaves began to usurp the yellows and the reds. The air, crisp and cold, had a strange nectar in it and its very breath was life. The sun lay in the heavens a ball of gold, and a fine haze, like a misty golden veil, hung over the forest. It was Indian summer.

Then Indian summer passed and winter, which was very early that year, came roaring down on Wareville. The autumn broke up in a cold rain which soon turned to snow. The wind swept out of the north-west, bitter and chill, and the desolate forest, every bough stripped of its leaves, moaned before the blast.

But it was cheerful, when the sleet beat upon the roof and the cold wind rattled the rude shutters, to sit before the big fires and watch them sparkle and blaze.

There was another reason why Henry should now begin to spend much of his time indoors. The Rev. Silas Pennypacker opened his school for the winter, and it was necessary for Henry to attend. Many of the pioneers who crossed the mountains from the Eastern States and founded the great Western outpost of the nation in Kentucky were men of education and cultivation, with a knowledge of books and the world. They did not intend that their children should grow up mere ignorant borderers, but they wished their daughters to have grace and manners and their sons to become men of affairs, fit to lead the vanguard of a mighty race. So a first duty in the wilderness was to found schools, and this they did.

The Reverend Silas was no lean and thin body, no hanger-on upon stronger men, but of fine girth and stature with a red face as round as the full moon, a glorious laugh and the mellowest voice in the colony. He was by repute a famous scholar who could at once give the chapter and text of any verse in the Bible and had twice read through the ponderous history of the French gentleman, M. Rollin. It was said, too, that he had nearly twenty volumes of some famous romances by a French lady, one Mademoiselle de Scudery, brought over the mountains in a box, but of this Henry and Paul could not speak with certainty, as a certain wooden cupboard in Mr. Pennypacker's house was always securely locked.

But the teacher was a favorite in the settlement with both men and women. A sight of his cheerful face was considered good enough to cure chills and fever, and for the matter of that he was an expert hand with both ax and rifle. His uses in Wareville were not merely mental and spiritual. He was at all times able and willing to earn his own bread with his own strong hands, though the others seldom permitted him to do so.

Henry entered school with some reluctance. Being nearly sixteen now, with an unusually powerful frame developed by a forest life, he was as large as an ordinary man and quite as strong. He thought he ought to have done with schools, and set up in man's estate but his father insisted upon another winter under Mr. Pennypacker's care and Henry yielded.

There were perhaps thirty boys and girls who sat on the rough wooden benches in the school and received tuition. Mr. Pennypacker did not undertake to guide them through many branches of learning, but what he taught he taught well. He, too, had the feeling that these boys and girls were to be the men and women who would hold the future of the West in their hands, and he intended that they should be fit. There were statesmen and generals among those red-faced boys on the benches, and the wives and mothers of others among the red-faced girls who sat near them, and he tried to teach them their duty as the heirs of a wilderness, soon to be the home of a great race.

Among his favorite pupils was Paul who had not Henry's eye and hand in the forest, but who loved books and the knowledge of men. He could follow the devious lines of history when Henry would much rather have been following the devious trail of a deer. Nevertheless, Henry persisted, borne up by the emulation of his comrade, and the knowledge that it was his last winter in school.

CHAPTER VI
THE VOICE OF THE WOODS

TO study now was the hardest task that Henry had ever undertaken. It was even easier to find food when he and Paul were unarmed and destitute in the forest. The walls of the little log house in which he sat inclosed him like a cell, the air was heavy and the space seemed to grow narrower and narrower. Then just when the task was growing intolerable he would look across the room and seeing the studious face of Paul bent over the big text of an ancient history, he would apply himself anew to his labor which consisted chiefly of "figures," a bit of the world's geography, and a little look into the history of England.

Mr. Pennypacker would neither praise nor blame, but often when the boy did not notice he looked critically at Henry. "I don't think your son will be a great scholar," he said once to Mr. Ware, "but he will be a Nimrod, a mighty hunter before men, and a leader in action. It's as well, for his is the kind that will be needed most and for a long time in this wilderness, and back there in the old lands, too."

"It is so," replied Mr. Ware, "the clouds do gather."

Involuntarily he looked toward the east, and Mr. Pennypacker's eyes followed him. But both remained silent upon that portion of their thoughts.

"Moreover I tell you for your comfort that the lad has a sense of duty," added the teacher.

Henry shot a magnificent stag with great antlers a few days later, and mounting the head he presented it to Mr. Pennypacker. But on the following day the master looked very grave and Henry and Paul tried to guess the cause. Henry heard that Ross had arrived the night before from the nearest settlement a hundred miles away, but had stayed only an hour, going to their second nearest neighbor distant one hundred and fifty miles. He brought news of some kind which only Mr. Ware, Mr. Upton, the teacher and three or four others knew. These were not ready to speak and Paul and Henry were well aware that nothing on earth could make them do so until they thought the time was fit.

It was a long, long morning. Henry had before him a map of the Empire of Muscovy but he saw little there. Instead there came between him and the page a vision of the beaver dam and the pool above it, now covered with a sheet of ice, and of the salt spring where the deer came to drink, and of a sheltered valley in which a herd of elk rested every night.

Mr. Pennypacker was singularly quiet that morning. It was his custom to call up his pupils and make them recite in a loud voice, but the hours passed and there were no recitations. The teacher seemed to be looking far away at something outside the schoolroom, and his thoughts followed his eyes. Henry by and by let his own roam as they would and he was in dreamland, when he was aroused by a sharp smack of the teacher's homemade ruler upon his homemade desk.

But the blow was not aimed at Henry or anybody in particular. It was an announcement to all the world in general that Mr. Pennypacker was about to speak on a matter of importance. Henry and Paul guessed at once that it would be about the news brought by Ross.

Mr. Pennypacker's face grew graver than ever as he spoke. He told them that when they left the east there was great trouble between the colonies and the mother country. They had hoped that it would pass away, but now, for the first time in many months, news had come across the mountains from their old home, and had entered the great forest. The troubles were not gone. On the contrary they had become worse. There had been fighting, a battle in which many had been killed, and a great war was begun. The colonies would all stand together, and no man could tell what the times would bring forth.

This was indeed weighty news. Though divided from their brethren in the east by hundreds of miles of mountain and forest the patriotism of the settlers in the wilderness burned with a glow all the brighter on that account. More than one young heart in that rude room glowed with a desire to be beside their countrymen in the far-off east, rifle in hand.

But Mr. Pennypacker spoke again. He said that there was now a greater duty upon them to hold the west for the union of the colonies. Their task was not merely to build homes for themselves, but to win the land that it might be homes for others. There were rumors that the savages would be used against them, that they might come down in force from the north, and therefore it was the part of everyone, whether man, woman or child to redouble his vigilance and caution. Then he adjourned school for the day.

The boys drew apart from their elders and discussed the great news. Henry's blood was on fire. The message from that little Massachusetts town, thrilled him as nothing in his life had done before. He had a vague idea of going there, and of doing what he considered his part, and he spoke to Paul about it, but Paul thought otherwise.

"Why, Henry!" he said. "We may have to defend ourselves here and we'll need you."

The people of Wareville knew little about the causes of the war and after this one message brought by Ross they heard no more of its progress. They might be fighting great battles away off there on the Atlantic coast, but no news came through the wall of woods. Wareville itself was peaceful, and around it curved the mighty forest which told nothing.

Mountains and forest alike lay under deep snow, and it was not likely that they would hear anything further until spring, because the winter was unusually cold and a man who ventured now on a long journey was braver than his fellows.

The new Kentuckians were glad that they had provided so well for winter. All the cupboards were full and there was no need for them now to roam the cold forests in search of game. They built the fires higher and watched the flames roar up the chimneys, while the little children rolled on the floor and grasped at the shadows.

Though but a bit of mankind hemmed in by the vast and frozen wilderness theirs was not an unhappy life by any means. The men and boys, though now sparing their powder and ball, still set traps for game and were not without reward. Often they found elk and deer, and once or twice a buffalo floundering in the deep snowdrifts, and these they added to the winter larder. They broke holes in the ice on the river and caught fish in abundance. They worked, too, about the houses, making more tables and benches and chairs and shelves and adding to their bodily comforts.

The great snow lasted about a month and then began to break up with a heavy rain which melted all the ice, but which could not carry away all the snow. The river rose rapidly and overflowed its banks but Wareville was safe, built high on the hill where floods could not reach. Warm winds followed the rain and the melting snow turned great portions of the forest into lakes. The trees stood in water a yard deep, and the aspect of the wilderness was gloomy and desolate. Even the most resolute of the hunters let the game alone at such a time. Often the warm winds would cease to blow when night came and then the great lagoons would be covered with a thin skim of ice which melted again the next day under the winds and the sun. All this brought chills and fever to Wareville and bitter herbs were sought for their cure. But the strong frame of Henry was impervious to the attacks and he still made daily journeys to his traps in the wet and steaming wilderness.

Henry was now reconciled to the schoolroom. It was to be his last term there and he realized with a sudden regret that it was almost at its end. He was beginning to feel the sense of responsibility, that he was in fact one of the units that must make up the state.

Despite these new ideas a sudden great longing lay hold of him. The winds from the south were growing warmer and warmer, all the snow and ice was gone long ago, faint touches of green and pink were appearing on grass and foliage and the young buds were swelling. Henry heard the whisper of these winds and every one of them called to him. He knew that he was wanted out there in the woods. He began to hate the sight of human faces, he wished to go alone into the wilderness, to see the deer steal among the trees and to hear the beaver dive into the deep waters. He felt himself a part of nature and he would breathe and live as nature did.

He grew lax in his tasks; he dragged his feet and there were even times when he was not hungry. When his mother noticed the latter circumstance she knew surely that the boy was ill, but her husband shrewdly said:

"Henry, the spring has come; take your rifle and bring us some fresh venison."

So Henry shouldered his rifle and went forth alone upon the quest, even leaving behind Paul, his chosen comrade. He did not wish human companionship that day, nor did he stop until he was deep in the wilderness. How he felt then the glory of living! The blood was flushing in his veins as the sap was rising in the trees around him. The world was coming forth from its torpor of winter refreshed and strengthened. He saw all about him the signs of new life--the tender young grass in shades of delicate green, the opening buds on the trees, and a subtle perfume that came on the edge of the Southern wind. Beyond him the wild turkeys on the hill were calling to each other.

He stood there a long time breathing the fresh breath of this new world, and the old desire to wander through illimitable forests and float silently down unknown rivers came over him. He would not feel the need of companionship on long wanderings. Nature would then be sufficient, talking to him in many tongues.

The wind heavy, with perfumes of the South, came over the hill and on its crest the wild turkeys were still clucking to each other. Henry, through sheer energy and flush of life, ran up the slope, and watched them as they took flight through the trees, their brilliant plumage gleaming in the sunshine.

It was the highest hill near Wareville and he stood a while upon its crest. The wilderness here circled around him, and, in the distance, it blended into one mass, already showing a pervading note of green with faint touches of pink bloom appearing here and there. The whole of it was still and peaceful with no sign of human life save a rising spire of smoke behind him that told where Wareville stood.

He walked on. Rabbits sprang out of the grass beside him and raced away into the thickets. Birds in plumage of scarlet and blue and gold shot like a flame from tree to tree. The forest, too, was filled with the melody of their voices, but Henry took no notice.

He paused a while at the edge of a brook to watch the silver sunfish play in the shallows, then he leaped the stream and went on into the deeper woods, a tall, lithe, strong figure, his eyes gazing at no one thing, the long slender-barreled rifle lying forgotten across his shoulder.

A great stag sprang up from the forest and stood for a few moments, gazing at him with expanding and startled eyes. Henry standing quite still returned the look, seeking to read the expression in the eyes of the deer.

Thus they confronted each other a half minute and then the stag turning fled through the woods. There was no undergrowth, and Henry for a long time watched the form of the deer fleeing down the rows of trees, as it became smaller and smaller and then disappeared.

All the forest glowed red in the setting sun when he returned home.

"Where is the deer?" asked his father.

"Why--why I forgot it!" said Henry in confused reply.

Mr. Ware merely smiled.

CHAPTER VII
THE GIANT BONES

ABOUT this time many people in Wareville, particularly the women and children began to complain of physical ills, notably lassitude and a lack of appetite; their food, which consisted largely of the game swarming all around the forest, had lost its savor. There was no mystery about it; Tom Ross, Mr. Ware and others promptly named the cause; they needed salt, which to the settlers of Kentucky was almost as precious as gold; it was obtained in two ways, either by bringing it hundreds of miles over the mountains from Virginia in wagons or on pack horses, or by boiling it out at the salt springs in the Indian-haunted woods.

They had neither the time nor the men for the long journey to Virginia, and they prepared at once for obtaining it at the springs. They had already used a small salt spring but the supply was inadequate, and they decided to go a considerable distance northward to the famous Big Bone Lick. Nothing had been heard in a long time of Indian war parties south of the Ohio, and they believed they would incur no danger. Moreover they could bring back salt to last more than a year.

When they first heard of the proposed journey, Paul Cotter pulled Henry to one side. They were just outside the palisade, and it was a beautiful day, in early spring. Already kindly nature was smoothing over the cruel scars made by the axes in the forest, and the village within the palisade began to have the comfortable look of home.

"Do you know what the Big Bone Lick is, Henry?" asked Paul eagerly.

"No," replied Henry, wondering at his chum's excitement.

"Why it's the most wonderful place in all the world!" said Paul, jumping up and down in his wish to tell quickly. "There was a hunter here last winter who spoke to me about it. I didn't believe him then, it sounded so wonderful, but Mr. Pennypacker says it's all true. There's a great salt spring, boiling out of the ground in the middle of a kind of marsh, and all around it, for a long distance, are piled hundreds of large bones, the bones of gigantic animals, bigger than any that walk the earth to-day."

"See here, Paul," said Henry scornfully, "you can't stuff my ears with mush like that. I guess you were reading one of the master's old romances, and then had a dream. Wake up, Paul!"

"It's true every word of it!"

"Then if there were such big animals, why don't we see 'em sometimes running through the forest?"

"My, they've all been dead millions of years and their bones have been preserved there in the marsh. They lived in another geologic era--that's what Mr. Pennypacker calls it--and animals as tall as trees strolled up and down over the land and were the lords of creation."

Henry puckered his lips and emitted a long whistle of incredulity.

"Paul," he said, reprovingly, "you do certainly have the gift of speech."

But Paul was not offended at his chum's disbelief.

"I'm going to prove to you, Henry, that it's true," he said. "Mr. Pennypacker says it's so, he never tells a falsehood and he's a scholar, too.

But you and I have got to go with the salt-makers, Henry, and we'll see it all. I guess if you look on it with your own eyes you'll believe it."

"Of course," said Henry, "and of course I'll go if I can."

A trip through the forest and new country to the great salt spring was temptation enough in itself, without the addition of the fields of big bones, and that night in both the Ware and Cotter homes, eloquent boys gave cogent reasons why they should go with the band.

"Father," said Henry, "there isn't much to do here just now, and they'll want me up at Big Bone Lick, helping to boil the salt and a lot of things."

Mr. Ware smiled. Henry, like most boys, seldom showed much zeal for manual labor. But Henry went on undaunted.

"We won't run any risk. No Indians are in Kentucky now and, father, I want to go awful bad."

Mr. Ware smiled again at the closing avowal, which was so frank. Just at that moment in another home another boy was saying almost exactly the same things, and another father ventured the same answer that Mr. Ware did, in practically the same words such as these:

"Well, my son, as it is to be a good strong company of careful and experienced men who will not let you get into any mischief, you can go along, but be sure that you make yourself useful."

The party was to number a dozen, all skilled foresters, and they were to lead twenty horses, all carrying huge pack saddles for the utensils and the invaluable salt. Mr. Silas Pennypacker who was a man of his own will announced that he was going, too. He puffed out his ruddy cheeks and said emphatically:

"I've heard from hunters of that place; it's one of the great curiosities of the country and for the sake of learning I'm bound to see it. Think of all the gigantic skeletons of the mastodon, the mammoth and other monsters lying there on the ground for ages!"

Henry and Paul were glad that Mr. Pennypacker was to be with them, as in the woods he was a delightful comrade, able always to make instruction entertaining, and the superiority of his mind appealed unconsciously to both of these boys who--each in his way--were also of superior cast.

They departed on a fine morning--the spring was early and held steady--and all Wareville saw them go. It was a brilliant little cavalcade; the horses, their heads up to scent the breeze from the fragrant wilderness, and the men, as eager to start, everyone with a long slender-barreled Kentucky rifle on his shoulder, the fringed and brilliantly colored deerskin hunting shirt falling almost to his knees, and, below that deerskin leggings and deerskin moccasins adorned with many-tinted beads. It was a vivid picture of the young West, so young, and yet so strong and so full of life, the little seed from which so mighty a tree was soon to grow.

All of them stopped again, as if by an involuntary impulse, at the edge of the forest, and waved their hands in another, and, this time, in a last good-by to the watchers at the fort. Then they plunged into the mighty wilderness, which swept away and away for unknown thousands of miles.

They talked for a while of the journey, of the things that they might see by the way, and of those that they had left behind, but before long conversation ceased. The spell of the dark and illimitable woods, in whose shade they marched, fell upon them, and there was no noise, but the sound of breathing and the tread of men and horses. They dropped, too, from the necessities of the path through the undergrowth, into Indian file, one behind the other.

Henry was near the rear of the line, the stalwart schoolmaster just in front of him, and his comrade Paul, just behind. He was full of thankfulness that he had been allowed to go on this journey. It all appealed to him, the tale that Paul told of the giant bones and the great salt spring, the dark woods full of mystery and delightful danger, and his own place among the trusted band, who were sent on such an errand. His heart swelled with pride and pleasure and he walked with a light springy step and with endurance equal to that of any of the men before him. He looked over his shoulder at Paul, whose face also was touched with enthusiasm.

"Aren't you glad to be along?" he asked in a whisper.

"Glad as I can be," replied Paul in the same whisper.

Up shot the sun showering golden beams of light upon the forest. The air grew warmer, but the little band did not cease its rapid pace northward until noon. Then at a word from Ross all halted at a beautiful glade, across which ran a little brook of cold water. The horses were tethered at the edge of the forest, but were allowed to graze on the young grass which was already beginning to appear, while the men lighted a small fire of last year's fallen brushwood, at the center of the glade on the bank of the brook.

"We won't build it high," said Ross, who was captain as well as guide, "an' then nobody in the forest can see it. There may not be an Indian south of the Ohio, but the fellow that's never caught is the fellow that never sticks his head in the trap."

"Sound philosophy! sound philosophy! your logic is irrefutable, Mr. Ross," said the schoolmaster.

Ross grinned. He did not know what "irrefutable" meant, but he did know that Mr. Pennypacker intended to compliment him.

Paul and Henry assisted with the fire. In fact they did most of the work, each wishing to make good his assertion that he would prove of use on the journey. It was a brief task to gather the wood and then Ross and Shif'less Sol lighted the fire, which they permitted merely to smolder. But it gave out ample heat and in a few minutes they cooked over it their venison and corn bread and coffee which they served in tin cups. Henry and Paul ate with the ferocious appetite that the march and the clean air of the wilderness had bred in them, and nobody restricted them, because the forest was full of game, and such skillful hunters and riflemen could never lack for a food supply.

Mr. Pennypacker leaned with an air of satisfaction against the up-thrust bough of a fallen oak.

"It's a wonderful world that we have here," he said, "and just to think that we're among the first white men to find out what it contains."

"All ready!" said Tom Ross, "then forward we go, we mustn't waste time by the way. They need that salt at Wareville."

Once more they resumed the march in Indian file and amid the silence of the woods. About the middle of the afternoon Ross invited Mr. Pennypacker and the two boys to ride three of the pack horses. Henry at first declined, not willing to be considered soft and pampered, but as the schoolmaster promptly accepted and Paul who was obviously tired did the same, he changed his mind, not because he needed rest, but lest Paul should feel badly over his inferiority in strength.

Thus they marched steadily northward, Ross leading the way, and Shif'less Sol who was lazy at the settlement, but never in the woods where he was inferior in knowledge and skill to Ross only, covering the rear. Each of these accomplished borderers watched every movement of the forest about him, and listened for every sound; he knew with the eye of second sight what was natural and if anything not belonging to the usual order of things should appear, he would detect it in a moment.

But they saw and heard nothing that was not according to nature: only the wind among the boughs, or the stamp of an elk's hoof as it fled, startled at the scent of man. The hostile tribes from north and south, fearful of the presence of each other, seemed to have deserted the great wilderness of Kentucky.

Henry noted the beauty of the country as they passed along; the gently rolling hills, the rich dark soil and the beautiful clear streams. Once they came to a river, too deep to wade, but all of them, except the schoolmaster, promptly took off their clothing and swam it.

"My age and my calling forbid my doing as the rest of you do," said the schoolmaster, "and I think I shall stick to my horse."

He rode the biggest of the pack horses, and when the strong animal began to swim, Mr. Pennypacker thrust out his legs until they were almost parallel with the animal's neck, and reached the opposite bank, untouched by a drop of water. No one begrudged him his dry and un-labored passage; in fact they thought it right, because a schoolmaster was mightily respected in the early settlements of Kentucky and they would have regarded it as unbecoming to his dignity to have stripped, and swum the river as they did.

Henry and Paul in their secret hearts did not envy the schoolmaster. They thought he had too great a weight of dignity to maintain and they enjoyed cleaving the clear current with their bare bodies. What! be deprived of the wilderness pleasures! Not they! The two boys did not remount, after the passage of the river, but, fresh and full of life, walked on with the others at a pace so swift that the miles dropped rapidly behind them. They were passing, too, through a country rarely trodden even by the red men; Henry knew it by the great quantities of game they saw; the deer seemed to look from every thicket, now and then a magnificent elk went crashing by, once a bear lumbered away, and twice small groups of buffalo were stampeded in the glades and rushed off, snorting through the undergrowth.

"They say that far to the westward on plains that seem to have no end those animals are to be seen in millions," said Mr. Pennypacker.

"It's so, I've heard it from the Indians," confirmed Ross the guide.

They stopped a little while before sundown, and as the game was so plentiful all around them, Ross said he would shoot a deer in order to save their dried meat and other provisions.

"You come with me, while the others are making the camp," he said to Henry.

The boy flushed with pride and gratification, and, taking his rifle, plunged at once into the forest with the guide. But he said nothing, knowing that silence would recommend him to Ross far more than words, and took care to bring down his moccasined feet without sound. Nor did he let the undergrowth rustle, as he slipped through it, and Ross regarded him with silent approval. "A born woodsman," he said to himself.

A mile from the camp they stopped at the crest of a little hill, thickly clad with forest and undergrowth, and looked down into the glade beyond. Here they saw several deer grazing, and as the wind blew from them toward the hunters they had taken no alarm.

"Pick the fat buck there on the right," whispered Ross to Henry.

Henry said not a word. He had learned the taciturnity of the woods, and leveling his rifle, took sure aim. There was no buck fever about him now, and, when his rifle cracked, the deer bounded into the air and dropped down dead. Ross, all business, began to cut up and clean the game, and with Henry's aid, he did it so skillfully and rapidly that they returned to the camp, loaded with the juicy deer meat, by the time the fire and everything else was ready for them.

Henry and Paul ate with eager appetites and when supper was over they wrapped themselves in their blankets and lay down before the fire under the trees. Paul went to sleep at once, but Henry did not close his eyes so soon. Far in the west he saw a last red bar of light cast by the sunken sun and the deep ruddy glow over the fringe of the forest. Then it suddenly passed, as if whisked away by a magic hand, and all the wilderness was in darkness. But it was only for a little while. Out came the moon and the stars flashed one by one into a sky of silky blue. A south wind lifting up itself sang a small sweet song among the branches, and Henry uttered a low sigh of content, because he lived in the wilderness, and because he was there in the depths of the forest on an important errand. Then he fell sound asleep, and did not awaken until Ross and the others were cooking breakfast.

A day or two later they reached the wonderful Big Bone Lick, and they approached it with the greatest caution, because they were afraid lest an errand similar to theirs might have drawn hostile red men to the great salt spring. But as they curved about the desired goal they saw no Indian sign, and then they went through the marsh to the spring itself.

Henry opened his eyes in amazement. All that the schoolmaster and Paul had told was true, and more. Acres and acres of the marsh lands were fairly littered with bones, and from the mud beneath other and far greater bones had been pulled up and left lying on the ground. Henry stood some of these bones on end, and they were much taller than he. Others he could not lift.

"The mastodon, the mammoth and I know not what," said Mr. Pennypacker in a transport of delight. "Henry, you and Paul are looking upon the remains of animals, millions of years old, killed perhaps in fights with others of their kind, over these very salt springs. There may not be another such place as this in all the world."

Mr. Pennypacker for the first day or two was absolutely of no help in making the salt, because he was far too much excited about the bones and the salt springs themselves.

"I can understand," said Henry, "why the animals should come here after the salt, since they crave salt just as we do, but it seems strange to me that salt water should be running out of the ground here, hundreds of miles from the sea."

"It's the sea itself that's coming up right at our feet," replied the schoolmaster thoughtfully. "Away back yonder, a hundred million years ago perhaps, so far that we can have no real conception of the time, the sea was over all this part of the world. When it receded, or the ground upheaved, vast subterranean reservoirs of salt water were left, and now, when the rain sinks down into these full reservoirs a portion of the salt water is forced to the surface, which makes the salt springs that are scattered over this part of the country. It is a process that is going on continually. At least, that's a plausible theory, and it's as good as any other."

But most of the salt-makers did not bother themselves about causes, and they accepted the giant bones as facts, without curiosity about their origin. Nor did they neglect to put them to use. By sticking them deep in the ground they made tripods of them on which they hung their kettles for boiling the salt water, and of others they devised comfortable seats for themselves. To such modern uses did the mastodon come! But to the schoolmaster and the two boys the bones were an unending source of interest, and in the intervals of labor, which sometimes were pretty long, particularly for Mr. Pennypacker, they were ever prowling in the swamp for a bone bigger than any that they had found before.

But the salt-making progressed rapidly. The kettles were always boiling and sack after sack was filled with the precious commodity. At night wild animals, despite the known presence of strange, new crea-tures, would come down to the springs, so eager were they for the salt, and the men rarely molested them. Only a deer now and then was shot for food, and Henry and Paul lay awake one night, watching two big bull buffaloes, not fifty yards away, fighting for the best place at a spring.

Ross and Shif'less Sol did not do much of the work at the salt-boiling, but they were continually scouting through the forest, on a labor no less important, watching for raiding war parties who otherwise might fall unsuspected upon the toilers. Henry, as a youth of great promise, was sometimes taken with them on these silent trips through the woods, and the first time he went he felt badly on Paul's account, because his comrade was not chosen also. But when he returned he found that his sympathy was wasted. Paul and the master were deeply absorbed in the task of trying to fit together some of the gigantic bones that is, to re-create the animal to which they thought the bones belonged, and Paul was far happier than he would have been on the scout or the hunt.

The day's work was ended and all the others were sitting around the camp fire, with the dying glow of the setting sun flooding the springs, the marshes and the camp fire, but Paul and the master toiled zealously at the gigantic figure that they had up-reared, supported partly with stakes, and bearing a remote resemblance to some animal that lived a few million years or so ago. The master had tied together some of the bones with withes, and he and Paul were now laboriously trying to fit a section of vertebrae into shape.

Shif'less Sol who had gone with Henry sat down by the fire, stuffed a piece of juicy venison into his mouth and then looked with eyes of wonder at the two workers in the cause of natural history.

"Some people 'pear to make a heap o' trouble for theirselves," he said, "now I can't git it through my head why anybody would want to work with a lot o' dead old bones when here's a pile o' sweet deer meat just waitin' an' beggin' to be et up."

At that moment the attempt of Paul and the schoolmaster to reconstruct a prehistoric beast collapsed. The figure that they had built up with so much care and labor suddenly slipped loose somewhere, and all the bones fell down in a heap. The master stared at them in disgust and exclaimed:

"It's no use! I can't put them together away out here in the wilderness!"

Then he stalked over to the fire, and taking a deer steak, ate hungrily. The steak was very tender, and gradually a look of content and peace stole over Mr. Pennypacker's face.

"At least," he murmured, "if it's hard to be a scholar here, one can have a glorious appetite, and it is most pleasant to gratify it."

As the dark settled down Ross said that in one day more they ought to have all the salt the horses could carry, and then it would be best to depart promptly and swiftly for Wareville. A half hour later all were asleep except the sentinel.

CHAPTER VIII
THE WILD TURKEY'S GOBBLE

HENRY had conducted himself so well on his first scout and, had shown such signs of efficiency that Ross concluded to take him again the next day. Henry's heart swelled with pride, and he was no longer worried about Paul, because he saw that the latter's interest and ambitions were not exactly the same as his own. Henry could not have any innate respect for heaps of "old bones," but if Paul and the master found them worthy of such close attention, they must be right.

Henry and Ross slipped away into the undergrowth, and Henry soon noticed that the guide's face, which was tense and preoccupied, seemed graver than usual. The boy was too wise to ask questions, but after they had searched through the forest for several hours Ross remarked in the most casual way:

"I heard the gobble of a wild turkey away off last night."

"Yes," said Henry, "there are lots of 'em about here. You remember the one I shot Tuesday?"

Ross did not reply just then, but in about five minutes he vouchsafed:

"I'm looking for the particular wild turkey I heard last night."

"Why that one, when there are so many, and how would you know him from the others if you found him?" asked Henry quickly, and then a deep burning flush of shame broke through the tan of his cheeks. He, Henry Ware, a rover of the wilderness to ask such foolish questions! A child of the towns would have shown as much sense. Ross who was looking covertly at him, out of the corner of his eye, saw the mounting blush, and was pleased. The boy had spoken impulsively, but he knew better.

"You understand, I guess," said Ross.

"Yes," replied Henry, "I know why you want to find that wild turkey, and I know why you said last night we ought to leave the salt springs just as soon as we can."

The smile on the face of the scout brightened. Here was the most promising pupil who had ever sat at his feet for instruction; and now they redoubled their caution, as their soundless bodies slipped through the undergrowth. Everywhere they looked for the trail of that wild turkey. It may be said that a turkey can and does fly in the air and leaves no trail, but Henry knew that the one for which they looked might leave no trail, but it did not fly in the air.

Time passed; noon and part of the afternoon were gone, and they were still curving in a great circle about the camp, when Ross, suddenly stopped beside a little brook, or branch, as he and his comrades always called them, and pointed to the soft soil at the edge of the water. Henry followed the long finger and saw the outline of a footstep.

"Our turkey has passed here."

The guide nodded.

"Most likely," he said, "and if not ours, then one of the same flock. But that footprint is three or four hours old. Come on, we'll follow this trail until it grows too warm."

The footsteps led down the side of the brook, and when they curved away from it Ross was able to trace them on the turf and through the undergrowth. A half mile from the start other footsteps joined them, and these were obviously made by many men, perhaps a score of warriors.

"You see," said Ross, "I guess they've just come across the Ohio or we wouldn't be left all these days b'il'n salt so peaceful, like as if there wasn't an Indian in the whole world."

Henry drew a deep breath. Like all who ventured into the West he expected some day to be exposed to Indian danger and attack, but it had been a vague thought. Even when they came north to the Big Bone Lick it was still a dim far-away affair, but now he stood almost in its presence. The Shawnees, whose name was a name of terror to the new settlements, were probably not a mile away. He felt tremors but they were not tremors of fear. Courage was an instinctive quality in him. Nature had put it there, when she fashioned him somewhat in the mold of the primitive man.

"Step lighter than you ever did afore in your life," said Ross, "an' bend low an' follow me. But don't you let a single twig nor nothin' snap as you pass."

He spoke in a sharp, emphatic whisper, and Henry knew that he considered the enemy near. But there was no need to caution the boy, in whom the primal man was already awakened. Henry bent far down, and holding his rifle before him in such a position that it could be used at a moment's warning, was following behind Ross so silently that the guide, hearing no sound, took an instant's backward glance. When he saw the boy he permitted another faint smile of approval to pass over his face.

They advanced about three-quarters of a mile and then at the crest of a hill thickly clothed in tall undergrowth the guide sank down and pointed with a long ominous forefinger.

"Look," he said.

Henry looked through the interlacing bushes and, for the second time in his life, gazed upon a band of red men. And as he looked, his blood for a moment turned cold. Perhaps thirty in number, they were sitting in a glade about a little fire. All of them had blankets of red or blue about them and they carried rifles. Their faces were hideous with war paint and their coarse black hair rose in the defiant scalp lock.

"Maybe they don't know that our men are at the Lick," said Ross, "or if they do they don't think we know they've come, an' they're planning for an attack to-night, when they could slip up on us sleepin'."

The guide's theory seemed plausible to Henry, but he said nothing. It did not become him to venture opinions before one who knew so much of the wilderness.

"It can't be more'n two o'clock," whispered Ross, "an' they'd attack about midnight. That gives us ten hours. Henry, the Lord is with us. Come."

He slid away through the bushes and Henry followed him. When they were a half mile from the Indian camp they increased their speed to an astonishing gait and in a half hour were at the Big Bone Lick.

"Have 'em to load up all the salt at once," said Ross to Shif'less Sol, "an' we must go kitin' back to Wareville as if our feet was greased."

Shif'less Sol shot him a single look of comprehension and Ross nodded. Then the shiftless one went to work with extraordinary diligence and the others imitated his speed. To the schoolmaster Ross breathed the one word "Shawnees," and Henry in a few sentences told Paul what he had seen.

Fortunately the precious salt was packed--they had no intention of deserting it, however close the danger--and it was quickly transferred to the backs of the horses along with the food for the way. In a little more than a half hour they were all ready and then they fled southward, Shif'less Sol, this time, leading the way, the guide Ross at the rear, eye and ear noticing everything, and every nerve attuned to danger.

The master cast back one regretful glance at his beloved giant bones, and then, with resignation, turned his face permanently toward the south and the line of retreat.

"O Henry," whispered Paul, half in delight, half in terror, "did you really see them?"

"Yes," replied Henry, "twenty or more of 'em, and an ugly lot they were, too, I can tell you, Paul. I believe we could whip 'em in a stand-up fight, though they are three to our one, but they know more of these woods than we do and then there's the salt; we've got to save what we've come for."

He sighed a little. He did not wholly like the idea of running away, even from a foe thrice as strong. Yet he could not question the wisdom of Ross and Shif'less Sol, and he made no protest.

The men looked after the heavily laden horses--nobody could ride except as a last resort--and southward they went in Indian file as they had come. Henry glanced around him and saw nothing that promised danger. It was only another beautiful afternoon in early spring. The forest glowed in the tender green of the young buds, and, above them arched the sky a brilliant sheet of unbroken blue. Never did a world look more attractive, more harmless, and it seemed incredible that these woods should contain men who were thirsting for the lives of other men. But he had seen; he knew; he could not forget that hideous circle of painted faces in the glade, upon which he and Ross had looked from the safe covert of the undergrowth.

"Do you think they'll follow us, Henry?" asked Paul.

"I don't know," replied Henry, "but it's mighty likely. They'll hang on our trail for a long time anyway."

"And if they overtake us, there'll be a fight?"

"Of course."

Henry, watching Paul keenly, saw him grow pale. But his lips did not tremble and that passing pallor failed to lower Paul in Henry's esteem. The bigger and stronger boy knew his comrade's courage and tenacity, and he respected him all the more for it, because he was perhaps less fitted than some others for the wild and dangerous life of the border.

After these few words they sank again into silence, and to Paul and the master the sun grew very hot. It was poised now at a convenient angle in the heavens, and poured sheaves of fiery rays directly upon them. Mr. Pennypacker began to gasp. He was a man of dignity, a teacher of youth, and it did not become him to run so fast from something that he could not see. Ross's keen eye fell upon him.

"I think you'd better mount one of the horses," he said; "the big bay there can carry his salt and you too for a while until you are rested."

"What! I ride, when everybody else is afoot!" exclaimed Mr. Pennypacker, indignantly.

"You're the only schoolmaster we have and we can't afford to lose you," said Ross without the suspicion of a grin.

Mr. Pennypacker looked at him, but he could not detect any change of countenance.

"Hop up," continued Ross, "it ain't any time to be bashful. Others of us may have to do it afore long."

Mr. Pennypacker yielded with a sigh, sprang lightly upon the horse, and then when he enjoyed the luxury of rest was glad that he had yielded. Paul, and one or two others took to the horses' backs later on, but

Henry continued the march on foot with long easy strides, and no sign of weakening. Ross noticed him more than once but he never made any suggestion to Henry that he ride; instead the faint smile of approval appeared once more on the guide's face.

The sun began to sink, the twilight came, and then night. Ross called a halt, and, clustered in the thickest shadows of the forest, they ate their supper and rested their tired limbs. No fire was lighted, but they sat there under the trees, hungrily eating their venison, and talking in the lowest of whispers.

Mr. Pennypacker was much dissatisfied. He had been troubled by the hasty flight and his dignity suffered.

"It is not becoming that white men should run away from an inferior race," he said.

"Maybe it ain't becomin', but it's safe," said Ross.

"At least we are far enough away now," continued the master, "and we might rest here comfortably until dawn. We haven't seen or heard a sign of pursuit."

"You don't know the natur' of the red warriors, Mr. Pennypacker," said the leader deferentially but firmly, "when they make the least noise then they're most dangerous. Now I'm certain sure that they struck our trail not long after we left Big Bone Lick, an' in these woods the man that takes the fewest risks is the one that lives the longest."

It was a final statement. In the present emergency the leader's authority was supreme. They rested about an hour with no sound save the shuffling feet of the horses which could not be kept wholly quiet; and then they started on again, not going so quickly now, because the night was dark, and they wished to make as little noise as possible, threshing about in the undergrowth.

Paul pressed up by the side of Henry.

"Do you think we shall have to go on all night, this way?" he asked. "Wasn't Mr. Pennypacker right, when he said we were out of danger?"

"No, the schoolmaster was wrong," replied Henry. "Tom Ross knows more about the woods and what is likely to happen in them than Mr. Pennypacker could know in all his life, if he were to live a thousand years. It's every man to his own trade, and it's Tom's trade that we need now."

After hearing these sage words of youth Paul asked no more questions, but he and Henry kept side by side throughout the night, that is, when neither of them was riding, because Henry, like all the others, now took turns on horseback. Twice they crossed small streams and once a larger one, where they exercised the utmost caution to keep their precious salt from getting wet. Fortunately the great pack saddles were a protection, and they emerged on the other side with both salt and powder dry.

When the night was thickest, in the long, dark hour just before the dawn, Henry and Paul, who were again side by side, heard a faint, distant cry. It was a low, wailing note that was not unpleasant, softened by the spaces over which it came. It seemed to be far behind them, but inclining to the right, and after a few moments there came another faint cry just like it, also behind them, but far to the left. Despite the soft, wailing note both Henry and Paul felt a shiver run through them. The strange low sound, coming in the utter silence of the night, had in it something ominous.

"It was the cry of a wolf," said Paul.

"And his brother wolf answered," said Henry.

Shif'less Sol was just behind them, and they heard him laugh, a low laugh, but full of irony. Paul wheeled about at once, his pride aflame at the insinuation that he did not know the wolf's long whine.

"Well, wasn't it a wolf--and a wolf that answered?" he asked.

"Yes, a wolf an' a wolf that answered," replied Shif'less Sol with sardonic emphasis, "but they had only four legs between 'em. Them was the signal cries of the Shawnees, an', as Tom has been tellin' you all the time, they're hot on our trail. It's a mighty lucky thing for us we didn't undertake to stay all night back there where we stopped."

Paul turned pale again, but his courage as usual came back. "Thank God it will be daylight soon," he murmured to himself, "and then if they overtake us we can see them."

Faint and far, but ominous and full of threat came the howl of the wolf again, first from the right and then from the left, and then from points between. Henry noticed that Ross and Shif'less Sol seemed to draw themselves together, as if they would make every nerve and muscle taut, and then his eyes shifted to Mr. Pennypacker, and seeing him, he knew at once that the master did not understand; he had not heard the words of Shif'less Sol.

"It seems that we are pursued by a pack of wolves instead of a war party," said Mr. Pennypacker. "At least we are numerous enough to beat off a lot of cowardly four-footed assailants."

Henry smiled from the heights of his superior knowledge.

"Those are not wolves, Mr. Pennypacker," he said, "those are the Shawnees calling to one another."

"Then, why in Heaven's name don't they speak their own language!" exclaimed the exasperated schoolmaster, "instead of using that which appertains only to the prowling beast?"

Henry, despite himself, was forced to smile, but he turned his face and hid the smile--he would not offend the schoolmaster whom he esteemed sincerely.

The dawn now began to brighten. The sun, a flaming red sword, cleft the gray veil, and then poured down a torrent of golden beams upon the vast, green wilderness of Kentucky. Henry, as he looked around upon the little band, realized what a tiny speck of human life they were in all those hundreds of miles of forest, and what risks they ran.

Ross gave the word to halt, and again they ate of cold food. While the others sat on fallen timber or leaned against tree trunks, Ross and Sol talked in low tones, but Henry could see that all their words were marked by the deepest earnestness. Ross presently turned to the men and said in tones of greatest gravity:

"All of you heard the howlin' just afore dawn, an' I guess all of you know it was not made by real wolves, but by Shawnees, callin' to each other an' directin' the chase of us. We've come fast, but they've come faster, an' I know that by noon we'll have to fight."

The schoolmaster's eyes opened in wonder.

"Do you really mean to say that they are overhauling us?" he asked.

"I shore do," replied Ross. "You see, they're better trained travelers for woods than we are, an' they are not hampered by anythin'."

Mr. Pennypacker said nothing more, but his lips suddenly closed tightly and his eyes flashed. In the great battle ground of the white man and the red man, called Kentucky, the early schoolmaster was as ready as any one else to fight.

Ross and Sol again consulted and then Ross said:

"We think that since we have to fight it would be better to fight when we are fresh and steady and in the best place we can find."

All the men nodded. They were tired of running and when Ross gave the word to stop again they did so promptly. The questioning eyes of both Ross and Sol roamed round the forest and finally and simultaneously the two uttered a low cry of pleasure. They had come into rocky ground and they had been ascending. Before them was a hill with a rather steep ascent, and dropping off almost precipitously on three sides.

"We couldn't find a better place," said Ross loud enough for all to hear. "It looks like a fort just made for us."

"But there is no line of retreat," objected the schoolmaster.

"We had a line of a retreat last night and all this mornin' an' we've been followin' it all the time," rejoined the leader. "Now we don't need it no more, but what we do need to do is to make a stan'-up fight, an' lick them fellers."

"And save our salt," added the master.

"Of course," said Ross emphatically. "We didn't come all these miles an' work all these days just to lose what we went so far after an' worked so hard for."

They retreated rapidly upon the great jutting peninsula of rocky soil, which fortunately was covered with a good growth of trees, and tethered the horses in a thick grove near the end.

"Now, we'll just unload our salt an' make a wall," said Ross with a trace of a smile. "They can shoot our salt as much as they please, just so they don't touch us."

The bags of salt were laid in the most exposed place across the narrowest neck of the peninsula and they also dragged up all the fallen tree trunks and boughs that they could find to help out their primitive fortification. Then they sat down to wait, a hard task for men, but hardest of all for two boys like Henry and Paul.

Two of the men went back with the horses to watch over them and also to guard against any possible attempt to scale the cliff in their rear, but the others lay close behind the wall of salt and brushwood. The sun swung up toward the zenith and shone down upon a beautiful world.

All the wilderness was touched with the tender young green of spring and nothing stirred but the gentle wind. The silky blue sky smiled over a scene so often enacted in early Kentucky, that great border battle ground of the white man and the red, the one driven by the desire for new and fertile acres that he might plow and call his own, the other by an equally fierce desire to retain the same acres, not to plow nor even to call his own, but that he might roam and hunt big game over them at will.

The great red eye of the sun, poised now in the center of the heavens, looked down at the white men crouched close to the earth behind their low and primitive wall, and then it looked into the forest at the red men creeping silently from tree to tree, all the eager ferocity of the man hunt on the face of everyone.

But Paul and Henry, behind their wall, saw nothing and heard nothing but the breathing of those near them. They fingered their rifles and through the crevices between the bags studied intently the woods in front of them, where they beheld no human being nor any trace of a foe. Henry looked from tree to tree, but he could see no flitting shadow. Where the patches of grass grew it moved only with the regular sweep of the breeze. He began to think that Ross and Sol must be mistaken. The warriors had abandoned the pursuit. He glanced at Ross, who was not a dozen feet away, and the leader's face was so tense, so eager and so earnest that Henry ceased to doubt, the man's whole appearance indicated the knowledge of danger, present and terrible.

Even as Henry looked, Ross suddenly threw up his rifle, and, apparently without aim, pulled the trigger. A flash of fire leaped from the long slender muzzle of blue steel, there was a sharp report like the swift lash of a whip, and then a cry, so terrible that Henry, strong as he was, shuddered in every nerve and muscle. The short high-pitched and agonizing shout died away in a wail and after it came silence, grim, deadly, but so charged with mysterious suspense that both Henry and Paul felt the hair lifting itself upon their heads. Henry had seen nothing, but he knew well what had happened.

"They've come and Ross has killed one of 'em," he whispered breathlessly to Paul.

"That yell couldn't mean anything else," said Paul trembling. "I'll hear it again every night for a year."

"I hope we'll both have a chance to hear it again every night for a year," said Henry with meaning.

The master crouched nearer to the boys. He was one of the bravest of the men and in that hour of danger and suspense his heart yearned over these two lads, his pupils, each a good boy in his own way. He felt that it was a part of his duty to get them safely back to Wareville and their parents, and he meant to fulfill the demands of his conscience.

"Keep down, lads," he said, touching Henry on his arm, "don't expose yourselves. You are not called upon to do anything, unless it comes to the last resort."

"We are going to do our best, of course, we are!" replied Henry with some little heat.

He resented the intimation that he could not perform a man's full duty, and Mr. Pennypacker, seeing that his feelings were touched, said no more.

A foreboding silence followed the death cry of the fallen warrior, but the brilliant sunshine poured down on the woods, just as if it were a glorious summer afternoon with no thought of strife in a human breast anywhere. Henry again searched the forest in front of them, and, although he could see nothing, he was not deceived now by this appearance of silence and peace. He knew that their foes were there, more thirsty than ever for their blood, because to the natural desire now was added the tally of revenge.

More than an hour passed, and then the forest in front of them burst into life. Rifles were fired from many points, the sharp crack blending into one continuous ominous rattle; little puffs of white smoke arose, whistling bullets buried themselves with a sighing sound in the bags of salt, and high above all rang the fierce yell, the war whoop of the Shawnees, the last sound that many a Kentucky pioneer ever heard.

The terrible tumult, and above all, the fierce cry of the warriors sent a thrill of terror through Paul and Henry, but their disciplined minds held their bodies firm, and they remained crouched by the primitive breastwork, ready to do their part.

"Steady, everybody! Steady!" exclaimed Ross in a loud sharp voice, every syllable of which cut through the tumult. "Don't shoot until you see something to shoot at, an' then make your aim true!"

Henry now began to see through the smoke dusky figures leaping from tree to tree, but always coming toward them. It was his impulse to fire, the moment a flitting figure appeared, gone the next instant like a shadow, but remembering Ross's caution and their terrible need he restrained himself although his finger already lay caressingly on the trigger. Around him the rifles had begun to crack. Ross and Sol were firing with slow deliberate aim, and then reloading with incredible swiftness, and down the line the others were doing likewise. Bullets were spattering into trunks and boughs, or burying themselves with a soft sigh in the salt, but Henry could not see that anybody was yet hurt.

He saw presently a dark figure passing from one tree to another and the passage was long enough for him to take a good aim at a hideously painted breast. He pulled the trigger and then involuntarily he shut his eyes--he was a hunter, but he had never hunted men before. When he looked again he saw a blur upon the ground, and despite himself and the fight for life, he shuddered. Paul beside him was now in a state of wild excitement. The smaller boy's nerves were not so steady and he was loading and firing almost at random. Finally he lifted himself almost unconsciously to his full height, but he was dragged down the next instant, as if he had been seized from below by a bear.

"Paul!" fiercely exclaimed the schoolmaster, all the instincts of a pedagogue rising within him, "if you jump up that way again exposing yourself to their bullets, I'll turn you over my knee right here, big as you are, and give you a licking that you'll remember all your life!"

The master was savagely in earnest and Paul did not jump up again. Henry fired once more, and a third time and the tumult rose to its height. Then it ceased so suddenly and so absolutely that the silence was appalling. The wind blew the smoke away, a few dark objects lay close to the ground among the trees before them, but not a sound came from the forest, and no flitting form was there.

CHAPTER IX
THE ESCAPE

HENRY and Paul, with their eyes at the crevices, stared and stared, but they saw only those dark, horrible forms lying close to the earth, and heard again the peaceful wind blowing among the peaceful trees. The savage army had melted away as if it had never been, and the dark objects might have been taken for stones or pieces of wood.

"We beat 'em off, an' nobody on our side has more'n a scratch," exclaimed Shif'less Sol jubilantly.

"That's so," said Ross, casting a critical eye down the line, "it's because we had a good position an' made ready. There's nothin' like takin' a thing in time. How're you, boys?"

"All right, but I've been pretty badly scared I can tell you," replied Paul frankly. "But we are not hurt, are we, Henry?"

"Thank God," murmured the schoolmaster under his breath, and then he said aloud to Ross: "I suppose they'll leave us alone now."

Ross shook his head.

"I wish I could say it," he replied, "but I can't. We've laid out four of 'em, good and cold, an' the Shawnees, like all the other redskins, haven't much stomach for a straightaway attack on people behind breastworks; I don't think they'll try that again, but they'll be up to new mischief soon. We must watch out now for tricks. Them's sly devils."

Ross was a wise leader and he gave food to his men, but he cautioned them to lie close at all times. Two or three bullets were fired from the forest but they whistled over their heads and did no damage. They seemed safe for the present, but Ross was troubled about the future, and particularly the coming of night, when they could not protect themselves so well, and the invaders, under cover of darkness, might slip forward at many points. Henry himself was man enough and experienced enough to understand the danger, and for the moment, he wondered with a kind of impersonal curiosity how Ross was going to meet it. Ross himself was staring at the heavens, and Henry, following his intent eyes, noticed a change in color and also that the atmosphere began to have a different feeling to his lungs. So much had he been engrossed by the battle, and so great had been his excitement, that such things as sky and air had no part then in his life, but now in the long dead silence, they obtruded themselves upon him.

The last wisp of smoke drifted away among the trees, and the sunlight, although it was mid-afternoon, was fading. Presently the skies were a vast dome of dull, lowering gray, and the breeze had a chill edge. Then the wind died and not a leaf or blade of grass in the forest stirred. Somber clouds came over the brink of the horizon in the southwest, and crept threateningly up the great curve of the sky. The air steadily darkened, and suddenly the dim horizon in the far southwest was cut by a vivid flash of lightning. Low thunder grumbled over the distant hills.

"It's a storm, an' it's to be a whopper," said Shif'less Sol.

"Ay," returned Ross, who had been back among the horses, "an' it may save us. All you fellows be sure to keep your powder dry."

There would be little danger of that fatal catastrophe, the wetting of the powder, as it was carried in polished horns, stopped securely, nor would there be any danger either of the salt being melted, as it was inclosed in bags made of deerskin, which would shed water.

"One of the men," continued Ross, "has found a big gully running down the back end of the hill, an' I think if we're keerful we can lead the horses to the valley that way. But just now, we'll wait."

Henry and Paul were watching, as if fascinated. They had seen before the great storms that sometimes sweep the Mississippi Valley, but the one preparing now seemed to be charged with a deadly power, far surpassing anything in their experience. It came on, too, with terrible swiftness. The thunder, at first a mere rumble, rose rapidly to crash after crash that stunned their ears. The livid flash of lightning that split the southwest like a flaming sword appeared and reappeared with such intensity that it seemed never to have gone. The wind rose and the forest groaned. From afar came a sullen roar, and then the great hurricane rushed down upon them.

"Lie flat!" shouted Ross.

All except four or five who held the struggling and frightened horses threw themselves upon the ground, and, although Henry and Paul hugged the earth, their ears were filled with the roar and scream of the wind, and the crackle of boughs and whole tree trunks snapped through, like the rattle of rifle fire. The forest in front of them was quickly filled with fallen trees, and fragments whistled over their heads, but fortunately they were untouched.

The great volley of wind was gone in a few moments, as if it were a single huge cannon shot. It whistled off to the eastward, but left in its path a trail of torn and fallen trees. Then in its path came the sweep of the great rain; the air grew darker, the thunder ceased to crash, the lightning died away, and the water poured down in sheets over the black and mangled forest.

"Now boys, we'll start," said Ross. "Them Shawnees had to hunt cover, an' they can't see us nohow. Up with them bags of salt!"

In an incredibly short time the salt was loaded on the pack horses and then they were picking their way down the steep and dangerous gully in the side of the hill. Henry, Paul and the master locked hands in the dark and the driving rain, and saved each other from falls. Ross and Sol seemed to have the eyes of cats in the dark and showed the way.

"My God!" murmured Mr. Pennypacker, "I could not have dreamed ten years ago that I should ever take part in such a scene as this!"

Low as he spoke, Henry heard him and he detected, too, a certain note of pride in the master's tone, as if he were satisfied with the manner in which he had borne himself. Henry felt the same satisfaction, although he could not deny that he had felt many terrors.

After much difficulty and some danger they reached the bottom of the hill unhurt, and then they sped across a fairly level country, not much troubled by undergrowth or fallen timber, keeping close together so that no one might be lost in the darkness and the rain, Ross, as usual, leading the line, and Shif'less Sol bringing up the rear. Now and then the two men called the names of the others to see that all were present, but beyond this precaution no word was spoken, save in whispers.

Henry and Paul felt a deep and devout thankfulness for the chance that had saved them from a long siege and possible death; indeed it seemed to them that the hand of God had turned the enemy aside, and in their thankfulness they forgot that, soaked to the bone, cold and tired, they were still tramping through the lone wilderness, far from Wareville.

The darkness and the pouring rain endured for about an hour, then both began to lighten, streaks of pale sky appeared in the east, and the

trees like cones emerged from the mist and gloom. All of the salt-work-
ers felt their spirits rise. They knew that they had escaped from the
conflict wonderfully well; two slight wounds, not more than the breaking of skin, and that was all. Fresh strength came to them, and as they
continued their journey the bars of pale light broadened and deepened,
and then fused into a solid blue dawn, as the last cloud disappeared and
the last shower of rain whisked away to the northward. A wet road lay
before them, the drops of water yet sparkling here and there, like myriads of beads. Ross drew a deep breath of relief and ordered a halt.

"The Shawnees could follow us again," he said, "but they know now
that they bit off somethin' a heap too tough for them to chaw, an' I
don't think they'll risk breaking a few more teeth on it, specially after
havin' been whipped aroun' by the storm as they must 'a been."

"And to think we got away and brought our salt with us, too!" said
Mr. Pennypacker.

Dark came soon, and Ross and Sol felt so confident they were safe
from another attack that they allowed a fire to be lighted, although they
were careful to choose the center of a little prairie, where the rifle shots
of an ambushed foe in the forest could not reach them.

It was no easy matter to light a fire, but Ross and Sol at last accomplished it with flint, steel and dry splinters cut from the under side of
fallen logs. Then when the blaze had taken good hold they heaped more
brushwood upon it and never were heat and warmth more grateful to
tired travelers.

Henry and Paul did not realize until then how weary and how very
wet they were. They basked in the glow, and, with delight watched the
great beds of coals form. They took off part of their clothing, hanging
it before the fire, and when it was dry and warm put it on again. Then
they served the rest the same way, and by and by they wore nothing

but warm garments.

"I guess two such terrible fighters as you," said Ross to Henry and Paul, "wouldn't mind a bite to eat. I've allers heard tell as how the Romans after they had fought a good fight with them Carthaginians or Macedonians or somebody else would sit down an' take some good grub into their insides, an' then be ready for the next spat."

"Will we eat? will we eat? Oh, try us, try us," chanted Henry and Paul in chorus, their mouths stretching simultaneously into wide grins, and Ross grinned back in sympathy.

The revulsion had come for the two boys. After so much danger and suffering, the sense of safety and the warmth penetrating their bones made them feel like little children, and they seized each other in a friendly scuffle, which terminated only when they were about to roll into the fire. Then they ate venison as if they had been famished. Afterwards, when they were asleep on their blankets before the fire, Ross said to Mr. Pennypacker:

"They did well, for youngsters."

"They certainly did, Mr. Ross," said the master. "I confess to you that there were times to-day when learning seemed to offer no consolation."

Ross smiled a little, and then his face quickly became grave.

"It's what we've got to go through out here," he said. "Every settlement will have to stand the storm."

A vigilant watch was kept all the long night but there was no sign of a second Shawnee attack. Ross had reckoned truly when he thought the Shawnees would not care to risk further pursuit, and the next day they resumed their journey, under a drying sun.

They were not troubled any more by Indian attacks, but the rest of the way was not without other dangers. The rivers were swollen by the spring rains, and they had great trouble in carrying the salt across on the swimming horses. Once Paul was swept down by a swift and powerful current, but Henry managed to seize and hold him until others came to the rescue. Men and boys alike laughed over their trials, because they felt now all the joy of victory, and their rapid march south amid the glories of spring, unfolding before them, appealed to the instincts of everyone in the band, the same instincts that had brought them from the East into the wilderness.

They were passing through the region that came to be known in later days as the Garden of Kentucky. Then it was covered with magnificent forest and now they threaded their way through the dense canebrake. Squirrels chattered in every tree top, deer swarmed in the woods, and the buffalo was to be found in almost every glen.

"I do not wonder," said the thoughtful schoolmaster, "that the Indian should be loath to give up such choice hunting grounds, but, fight as cunningly and bravely as he will, his fate will come."

But Henry, with only the thoughts of youth, could not conceive of the time when the vast wilderness should be cut down and the game should go. He was concerned only with the present and the words of Mr. Pennypacker made upon him but a faint and fleeting impression.

At last on a sunny morning, whole, well fed, with their treasure preserved, and all fresh and courageous, they approached Wareville. The hearts of Henry and Paul thrilled at the signs of white habitation. They saw where the ax had bitten through a tree, and they came upon broad trails that could be made only by white men, going to their work, or hunting their cattle.

But it was Paul who showed the most eagerness. He was wholehearted in his joy. Wareville then was the only spot on earth for him. But Henry turned his back on the wilderness with a certain reluctance.

A primitive strain in him had been awakened. He was not frightened now. The danger of the battle had aroused in him a certain wild emotion which repeated itself and refused to die, though days had passed. It seemed to him at times that it would be a great thing to live in the forest, and to have knowledge and wilderness power surpassing those even of Shif'less Sol or Ross. He had tasted again the life of the primitive man and he liked it.

Mr. Pennypacker was visibly joyful. The wilderness appealed to him in a way, but he considered himself essentially a man of peace, and Wareville was becoming a comfortable abode.

"I have had my great adventure," he said, "I have helped to fight the wild men, and in the days to come I can speak boastfully of it, even as the great Greeks in Homer spoke boastfully of their achievements, but once is enough. I am a man of peace and years, and I would fain wage the battles of learning rather than those of arms."

"But you did fight like a good 'un when you had to do it, schoolmaster," said Ross.

Mr. Pennypacker shook his head and replied gravely:

"Tom, you do right to say 'when I had to do it,' but I mean that I shall not have to do it any more."

Ross smiled. He knew that the schoolmaster was one of the bravest of men.

Now they came close to Wareville. From a hill they saw a thin, blue column of smoke rising and then hanging like a streamer across the clear blue sky.

"That comes from the chimneys of Wareville," said Ross, "an' I guess she's all right. That smoke looks kinder quiet, as if nothin' out of the way had happened."

They pressed forward with renewed speed, and presently a shout came from the forest. Two men ran to meet them, and rejoiced at the sight of the men unharmed, and every horse heavily loaded with salt. Then it was a triumphal procession into Wareville, with the crowd about them thickening as they neared the gates. Henry's mother threw her arms about his neck, and his father grasped him by the hand. Paul was in the center of his own family, completely submerged, and all the space within the palisade resounded with joyous laugh and welcome, which became all the more heartfelt, when the schoolmaster told of the great danger through which they had passed.

That evening, when they sat around the low fire in his father's home--the spring nights were yet cool--Henry had to repeat the story of the salt-making and the great adventure with the Shawnees. He grew excited as he told of the battle and the storm, his face flushed, his eyes shot sparks, and, as Mrs. Ware looked at him, she realized, half in pride, half in terror, that she was the mother of a hunter and warrior.

CHAPTER X
THE CAVE DUST

THE great supply of salt brought by Ross and his men was welcome to Wareville, as the people had begun to suffer for it, but they would have enough now to last them a full year, and a year was a long time to look ahead. Great satisfaction was expressed on that score, but the news that a Shawnee war party was in Kentucky and had chased them far southward caused Mr. Ware and other heads of the village to look very grave and to hold various councils.

As a result of these talks the palisade was strengthened with another row of strong stakes, and they took careful stock of their supplies of ammunition. Lead they had in plenty, but powder was growing scarce. A fresh supply had been expected with a new band of settlers from Virginia but the band had failed to come, and the faces of the leaders grew yet graver, when they looked at the dwindling supply, and wondered how it could be replenished for the dire need that might arise. It was now that Mr. Pennypacker came forward with a suggestion and he showed how book learning could be made of great value, even in the wilderness.

"You will recall," he said to Mr. Ware and Mr. Upton, and other heads of the settlement, "that some of our hunters have reported the existence of great caves to the southwestward and that they have brought back from them wonderful stalactites and stalagmites and also dust from the cave floors. I find that this dust is strongly impregnated with niter; from niter we obtain saltpeter and from saltpeter we make gunpowder. We need not send to Virginia for our powder, we can make it here in Kentucky for ourselves."

"Do you truly think so, Mr. Pennypacker?" asked Mr. Ware, doubtfully.

"Think so! I know so," replied the schoolmaster in sanguine tones. "Why, what am I a teacher for if I don't know a little of such things? And even if you have doubts, think how well the experiment is worth trying. Situated as we are, in this wild land, powder is the most precious thing on earth to us."

"That is true! that is true!" said Mr. Ware with hasty emphasis. "Without it we shall lie helpless before the Indian attack, should it come. If, as you say, this cave dust contains the saltpeter, the rest will be easy."

"It contains saltpeter and the rest *will* be easy!"

"Then, you must go for it. Ross and Sol and a strong party must go with you, because we cannot run the risk of losing any of you through the Indians."

"I am sure," said Mr. Pennypacker, "that we shall incur no danger from Indians. The region of the great caves lies farther south than Wareville and the Southern Indians, who are less bold than the Northern tribes, are not likely to come again into Kentucky. The hunters say that Indians have not been in that particular region for years."

"Yes, I think you are right," said Mr. Ware, "but be careful anyhow."

Henry, when he heard of the new expedition, was wild to go, but his parents, remembering the great danger of the journey to the salt licks, were reluctant with their permission. Then Ross interceded effectively.

"The boy is just fitted for this sort of work," he said. "He isn't in love with farming, he's got other blood in him, but down there he will be just about the best man that Wareville has to send, an' there won't be any Indians."

There was no reply to such an argument, because in the border settlements the round peg must go in the round hole; the conditions of survival demanded no surplusage and no waste.

When Paul heard that Henry was to go he gave his parents no rest, and when Mr. Pennypacker, whose favorite he was, seconded his request, on the ground that he would need a scholar with him the permission had to be granted.

Rejoicing, the two boys set forth with the others, the dangers of the Shawnee battle and their terrors already gone from their minds. They would meet no Indians this time, and the whole powder-making expedition would be just one great picnic. The summer was now at hand, and the forests were an unbroken mass of brilliant green. In the little spaces of earth where the sunlight broke through, wild flowers, red, blue, pink and purple peeped up and nodded gayly, when the light winds blew. Game abounded, but they killed only enough for their needs, Ross saying it was against the will of God to shoot a splendid elk or buffalo and leave him to rot, merely for the pleasure of the killing.

After a while they forded a large river, passed out of the forests, and came into a great open region, to which they gave the name of Barrens, not because it was sterile, but because it was bare of trees. Henry, at first, thought it was the land of prairies, but Ross, after examining it minutely, said that if left to nature it would be forested. It was his theory that the Indians in former years had burned off the young tree growth repeatedly in order to make great grazing grounds for the big game. Whether his supposition was true or not, and Henry thought it likely to be true, the Barrens were covered with buffalo, elk and deer. In fact they saw buffalo in comparatively large numbers for the first time, and once they looked upon a herd of more than a hundred, grazing in the rich and open meadows. Panthers attracted by the quantity of game upon which they could prey screamed horribly at night, but the flaming camp fires of the travelers were sufficient to scare them away.

All these things, the former salt-makers, and powder-makers that hoped to be, saw only in passing. They knew the value of time and they hastened on to the region of great caves, guided this time by one of their hunters, Jim Hart, although Ross as usual was in supreme command. But Hart had spent some months hunting in the great cave region and his report was full of wonders.

"I think there are caves all over, or rather, under this country that the Indians call Kaintuckee," he said, "but down in this part of it they're the biggest."

"You are right about Kentucky being a cave region," said the school-master, "I think most of it is underlaid with rock, anywhere from five thousand to ten thousand feet thick, and in the course of ages, through geological decay or some kindred cause, it has become crisscrossed with holes like a great honeycomb."

"I'm pretty sure about the caves," said Ross, "but what I want to know is about this peter dirt."

"We'll find it and plenty of it," replied the master confidently. "That sample was full of niter, and when we leach it in our tubs we shall have the genuine saltpeter, explosive dust, if you choose to call it, that is the solution of gunpowder."

"Which we can't do without," said Henry.

They passed out of the Barrens, and entered a region of high, rough hills, and narrow little valleys. Hills and valleys alike were densely clothed with forest.

Hart pointed to several, large holes in the sides of the hills, always at or near the base and said they were the mouths of caves.

"But the big one, in which I got the peter dirt is farther on," he said.

They came to the place he had in mind, just as the twilight was falling, a hole, a full man's height at the bottom of a narrow valley, but leading directly into the side of the circling hill that inclosed the bowl-like depression. Henry and Paul looked curiously at the black mouth and they felt some tremors at the knowledge that they were to go in there, and to remain inside the earth for a long time, shut from the light of day. It was the dark and not the fear of anything visible, that frightened them.

But they made no attempt to enter that evening, although night would be the same as day in the cave. Instead they provided for a camp, as the horses and a sufficient guard would have to remain outside. The valley itself was an admirable place, since it contained pasturage for the horses, while at the far end was a little stream of water, flowing out of the hill and trickling away through a cleft into another and slightly lower valley.

After tethering the horses, they built a fire near the cave mouth and sat down to cook, eat, rest and talk.

"Ain't there danger from bad air in there?" asked Ross. "I've heard tell that sometimes in the ground air will blow all up, when fire is touched to it, just like a bar'l o' gunpowder."

"The air felt just as fresh an' nice as daylight when I went in," said

Hart, "an' if it comes to that it will be better than it is out here because it's allus even an' cool."

"It is so," said the master meditatively. "All the caves discovered so far in Kentucky have fresh pure air. I do not undertake to account for it."

That night they cut long torches of resinous wood, and early the next morning all except two, who were left to guard the horses, entered the cave, led by Hart, who was a fearless man with an inquiring mind. Everyone carried a torch, burning with little smoke, and after they had passed the cave mouth, which was slightly damp, they came to a perfectly dry passage, all the time breathing a delightfully cool and fresh air, full of vigor and stimulus.

Paul and Henry looked back. They had come so far now that the light of day from the cave mouth could not reach them, and behind them was only thick impervious blackness. Before them, where the light of the torches died was the same black wall, and they themselves were only a little island of light. But they could see that the cave ran on before them, as if it were a subterranean, vaulted gallery, hewed out of the stone by hands of many Titans! Henry held up his torch, and from the roof twenty feet above his head the stone flashed back multicolored and glittering lights. Paul's eyes followed Henry's and the gleaming roof appealed to his sensitive mind.

"Why, it's all a great underground palace!" he exclaimed, "and we are the princes who are living in it!"

Hart heard Paul's enthusiastic words and he smiled.

"Come here, Paul," he said, "I want to show you something."

Paul came at once and Hart swung the light of his torch into a dark cryptlike opening from the gallery.

"I see some dim shapes lying on the floor in there, but I can't tell exactly what they are," said Paul.

"Come into this place itself."

Paul stepped into the crypt, and Hart with the tip of his moccasined toe gently moved one of the recumbent forms. Paul could not repress a little cry as he jumped back. He was looking at the dark, withered face of an Indian, that seemed to him a thousand years old.

"An' the others are Indians, too," said Hart. "An' they needn't trouble us. God knows how long they've been a-layin' here where their friends brought 'em for burial. See the bows an' arrows beside 'em. They ain't like any that the Indians use now."

"And the dry cave air has preserved them, for maybe two or three hundred years," said the schoolmaster. "No, their dress and equipment do not look like those of any Indians whom I have seen."

"Let's leave them just as they are," said Paul.

"Of course," said Ross, "it would be bad luck to move 'em."

They went on farther into the cave, and found that it increased in grandeur and beauty. The walls glittered with the light of the torches, the ceiling rose higher, and became a great vaulted dome. From the roof hung fantastic stalactites and from the floor stalagmites equally fantastic shot up to meet them. Slow water fell drop by drop from the point of the stalactite upon the point of the stalagmite.

"That has been going on for ages," said the schoolmaster, "and the same drop of water that leaves some of its substance to form the stalactite, hanging from the roof, goes to form the stalagmite jutting up from the floor. Come, Paul, here's a seat for you. You must rest a bit."

They beheld a rock formation almost like a chair, and, Paul sitting down in it, found it quite comfortable. But they paused only a moment, and then passed on, devoting their attention now to the cave dust, which was growing thicker under their feet. The master scooped up handfuls of it and regarded it attentively by the close light of his torch.

"It's the genuine peter dust!" he exclaimed exultantly. "Why, we can make powder here as long as we care to do so."

"You are sure of it, master?" asked Ross anxiously.

"Sure of it!" replied Mr. Pennypacker. "Why, I know it. If we stayed here long enough we could make a thousand barrels of gunpowder, good enough to kill any elk or buffalo or Indian that ever lived."

Ross breathed a deep sigh of relief. He had had his doubts to the last, and none knew better than he how much depended on the correctness of the schoolmaster's assertion.

"There seems to be acres of the dust about here," said Ross, "an' I guess we'd better begin the makin' of our powder at once."

They went no farther for the present, but carried the dust in, sack after sack, to the mouth of the cave. Then they leached it, pouring water on it in improvised tubs, and dissolving the niter. This solution they boiled down and the residuum was saltpeter or gunpowder, without which no settlement in Kentucky could exist.

The little valley now became a scene of great activity. The fires were always burning and sack after sack of gunpowder was laid safely away in a dry place. Henry and Paul worked hard with the others, but they never passed the crypt containing the mummies, without a little shudder. In some of the intervals of rest they explored portions of the cave, although they were very cautious. It was well that they were so as one day Henry stopped abruptly with a little gasp of terror. Not five feet before him appeared the mouth of a great perpendicular well. It was perfectly round, about ten feet across, and when Henry and Paul held their torches over the edge, they could see no bottom. Henry shouted, throwing his voice as far forward as possible, but only a dull, distant echo came back.

"We'll call that the Bottomless Pit," he said.

"Bottomless or not, it's a good thing to keep out of," said Paul. "It gives me the shudders, Henry, and I don't think I'll do much more exploring in this cave."

In fact, the gunpowder-making did not give them much more chance, and they were content with what they had already seen. The cave had many wonders, but the sunshine outside was glorious and the vast mass of green forest was very restful to the eye. There was hunting to be done, too, and in this Henry bore a good part, he and Ross supplying the fresh meat for their table.

A fine river flowed not two miles away and Paul installed himself as chief fisherman, bringing them any number of splendid large fish, very savory to the taste. Ross and Sol roamed far among the woods, but they reported absolutely no Indian sign.

"I don't believe any of the warriors from either north or south have been in these parts for years," said Ross.

"Luckily for us," added Mr. Pennypacker, "I don't want another such retreat as that we had from the salt springs."

Ross's words came true. The powder-making was finished in peace, and the journey home was made under the same conditions. At Wareville there was a shout of joy and exultation at their arrival. They felt that they could hold their village now against any attack, and Mr. Pennypacker was a great man, justly honored among his people. He had shown them how to make powder, which was almost as necessary to them as the air they breathed, and moreover they knew where they could always get materials needed for making more of it.

Truly learning was a great thing to have, and they respected it.

CHAPTER XI
THE FOREST SPELL

WHEN the adventurers returned the rifle and ax were laid aside at Wareville, for the moment, because the supreme test was coming. The soil was now to respond to its trial, or to fail. This was the vital question to Wareville. The game, in the years to come, must disappear, the forest would be cut down, but the qualities of the earth would remain; if it produced well, it would form the basis of a nation, if not, it would be better to let all the work of the last year go and seek another home elsewhere.

But the settlers had little doubt. All their lives had been spent close to the soil, and they were not to be deceived, when they came over the mountains in search of a land richer than any that they had tilled before. They had seen its blackness, and, plowing down with the spade, they had tested its depth. They knew that for ages and ages leaf and bough, falling upon it, had decayed there and increased its fertility, and so they awaited the test with confidence.

The green young shoots of the wheat, sown before the winter, were the first to appear, and everyone in Wareville old enough to know the importance of such a manifestation went forth to examine them. Mr. Ware, Mr. Upton and Mr. Pennypacker held solemn conclave, and the final verdict was given by the schoolmaster, as became a man who might not be so strenuous in practice as the others, but who nevertheless was more nearly a master of theory.

"The stalks are at least a third heavier than those in Maryland or Virginia at the same age," he said, "and we can fairly infer from it that the grain will show the same proportion of increase. I take a third as a most conservative estimate; it is really nearer a half. Wareville can, with reason, count upon twenty-five bushels of wheat to the acre, and it is likely to go higher."

It was then no undue sense of elation that Wareville felt, and it was shared by Henry and Paul, and even young Lucy Upton.

"It will be a rich country some day when I'm an old, old woman," she said to Henry.

"It's a rich country now," replied he proudly, "and it will be a long, long time before you are an old woman."

They began now to plow the ground cleared the autumn before--"new ground" they called it--for the spring planting of maize. This, often termed "Indian corn" but more generally known by the simple name corn, was to be their chief crop, and the labor of preparation, in which Henry had his full share, was not light. Their plows were rude, made by themselves, and finished with a single iron point, and the ground, which had supported the forest so lately, was full of roots and stumps. So the passage of the plow back and forth was a trial to both the muscles and the spirit. Henry's body became sore from head to foot, and by and by, as the spring advanced and the sun grew hotter, he looked longingly at the shade of the forest which yet lay so near, and thought of the deep, cool pools and the silver fish leaping up, until their scales shone like gold in the sunshine, and of the stags with mighty antlers coming down to drink. He was sorry for the moment that he was so large and strong and was so useful with plow and hoe. Then he might be more readily excused and could take his rifle and seek the depths of the forest, where everything grew by nature's aid alone, and man need not work, unless the spirit moved him to do so.

They planted the space close around the fort in gardens and here after the ground was "broken up" or plowed, the women and the girls, all tall and strong, did the work.

The summer was splendid in its promise and prodigal in its favors. The rains fell just right, and all that the pioneers planted came up in abundance. The soil, so kind to the wheat, was not less so to the corn and the gardens. Henry surveyed with pride the field of maize cultivated by himself, in which the stalks were now almost a foot high, looking in the distance like a delicate green veil spread over the earth. His satisfaction was shared by all in Wareville because after this fulfillment of the earth's promises, they looked forward to continued seasons of plenty.

When the heavy work of planting and cultivating was over and there was to be a season of waiting for the harvest, Henry went on the great expedition to the Mississippi.

In the party were Ross, Shif'less Sol, the schoolmaster, Henry and Paul. Wareville had no white neighbor near and all the settlements lay to the north or east. Beyond them, across the Ohio, was the formidable cloud of Indian tribes, the terror of which always overhung the settlers. West of them was a vast waste of forest spreading away far beyond the Mississippi, and, so it was supposed, inhabited only by wild animals. It was thought well to verify this supposition and therefore the exploring expedition set out.

Each member of the party carried a rifle, hunting knife and ammunition, and in addition they led three pack horses bearing more ammunition, their meal, jerked venison and buffalo meat. This little army expected to live upon the country, but it took the food as a precaution.

They started early of a late but bright summer morning, and Henry found all his old love of the wilderness returning. Now it would be gratified to the full, as they should be gone perhaps two months and would pass through regions wholly unknown. Moreover he had worked hard for a long time and he felt that his holiday was fully earned; hence there was no flaw in his hopes.

It required but a few minutes to pass through the cleared ground, the new fields, and reach the forest and as they looked back they saw what a slight impression they had yet made on the wilderness. Wareville was but a bit of human life, nothing more than an islet of civilization in a sea of forest.

Five minutes more of walking among the trees, and then both Wareville and the newly opened country around it were shut out. They saw only the spire of smoke that had been a beacon once to Henry and Paul, rising high up, until it trailed off to the west with the wind, where it lay like a whiplash across the sky. This, too, was soon lost as they traveled deeper into the forest, and then they were alone in the wilderness, but without fear.

"When we were able to live here without arms or ammunition it's not likely that we'll suffer, now is it?" said Paul to Henry.

"Suffer!" exclaimed Henry. "It's a journey that I couldn't be hired to miss."

"It ought to be enjoyable," said Mr. Pennypacker; "that is, if our relatives don't find it necessary to send into the Northwest, and try to buy back our scalps from the Indian tribes."

But the schoolmaster was not serious. He had little fear of Indians in the western part of Kentucky, where they seldom ranged, but he thought it wise to put a slight restraint upon the exuberance of youth.

They camped that night about fifteen miles from Wareville under the shadow of a great, overhanging rock, where they cooked some squirrels that the shiftless one shot, in a tall tree. The schoolmaster upon this occasion constituted himself cook.

"There is a popular belief," he said when he asserted his place, "that a man of books is of no practical use in the world. I hereby intend to give a living demonstration to the contrary."

Ross built the fire, and while the schoolmaster set himself to his task, Henry and Paul took their fish hooks and lines and went down to the creek that flowed near. It was so easy to catch perch and other fish that there was no sport in it, and as soon as they had enough for supper and breakfast they went back to the fire where the tempting odors that arose indicated the truth of the schoolmaster's assertion. The squirrels were done to a turn, and no doubt of his ability remained.

Supper over, they made themselves beds of boughs under the shadow of the rock, while the horses were tethered near. They sank into dreamless sleep, and it was the schoolmaster who awakened Paul and Henry the next morning.

They entered that day a forest of extraordinary grandeur, almost clear of undergrowth and with illimitable rows of mighty oak and beech trees. As they passed through, it was like walking under the lofty roof of an immense cathedral. The large masses of foliage met overhead and shut out the sun, making the space beneath dim and shadowy, and sometimes it seemed to the explorers that an echo of their own footsteps came back to them.

Henry noted the trees, particularly the beeches which here grow to finer proportions than anywhere else in the world, and said he was glad that he did not have to cut them down and clear the ground, for the use of the plow.

After they passed out of this great forest they entered the widest stretch of open country they had yet seen in Kentucky, though here and there they came upon patches of bushes.

"I think this must have been burned off by successive forest fires," said Ross, "Maybe hunting parties of Indians put the torch to it in order to drive the game."

Certainly these prairies now contained an abundance of animal life. The grass was fresh, green and thick everywhere, and from a hill the explorers saw buffalo, elk, and common deer grazing or browsing on the bushes.

As the game was so abundant Paul, the least skillful of the party in such matters, was sent forth that evening to kill a deer and this he triumphantly accomplished to his own great satisfaction. They again slept in peace, now under the low-hanging boughs of an oak, and continued the next day to the west. Thus they went on for days.

It was an easy journey, except when they came to rivers, some of which were too deep for fording, but Ross had made provision for them. Perched upon one of the horses was a skin canoe, that is, one made of stout buffalo hide to be held in shape by a slight framework of wood on the inside, such as they could make at any time. Two or three trips in this would carry themselves and all their equipment over the stream while the horses swam behind.

They soon found it necessary to put their improvised canoe to use as they came to a great river flowing in a deep channel. Wild ducks flew about its banks or swam on the dark-blue current that flowed quietly to the north. This was the Cumberland, though nameless then to the travelers, and its crossing was a delicate operation as any incautious movement might tip over the skin canoe, and, while they were all good swimmers, the loss of their precious ammunition could not be taken as anything but a terrible misfortune.

Traveling on to the west they came to another and still mightier river, called by the Indians, so Ross said, the Tennessee, which means in their language the Great Spoon, so named because the river bent in curves like a spoon. This river looked even wilder and more picturesque than the Cumberland, and Henry, as he gazed up its stream, wondered if the white man would ever know all the strange regions through which it flowed. Vast swarms of wild fowl, as at the Cumberland, floated upon its waters or flew near and showed but little alarm as they passed. When they wished food it was merely to go a little distance and take it as one walks to a cupboard for a certain dish.

Now, the aspect of the country began to change. The hills sank. The streams ceased to sparkle and dash helter-skelter over the stones; instead they flowed with a deep sluggish current and always to the west. In some the water was so nearly still that they might be called lagoons. Marshes spread out for great distances, and they were thronged with millions of wild fowl. The air grew heavier, hotter and damper.

"We must be approaching the Mississippi," said Henry, who was quick to draw an inference from these new conditions.

"It can't be very far," replied Ross, "because we are in low country now, and when we get into the lowest the Mississippi will be there."

All were eager for a sight of the great river. Its name was full of magic for those who came first into the wilderness of Kentucky. It seemed to them the limits of the inhabitable world. Beyond stretched vague and shadowy regions, into which hunters and trappers might penetrate, but where no one yet dreamed of building a home. So it was with some awe that they would stand upon the shores of this boundary, this mighty stream that divided the real from the unreal.

But traveling was now slow. There were so many deep creeks and lagoons to cross, and so many marshes to pass around that they could not make many miles in a day. They camped for a while on the highest hill that they could find and fished and hunted. While here they built themselves a thatch shelter, acting on Ross's advice, and they were very glad that they did so, as a tremendous rain fell a few days after it was finished, deluging the country and swelling all the creeks and lagoons. So they concluded to stay until the earth returned to comparative dryness again in the sunshine, and meanwhile their horses, which did not stand the journey as well as their masters, could recuperate.

Two days after they resumed the journey, they stood on the low banks of the Mississippi and looked at its vast yellow current flowing in a mile-wide channel, and bearing upon its muddy bosom, bushes and trees, torn from slopes thousands of miles away. It was not beautiful, it was not even picturesque, but its size, its loneliness and its desolation gave it a somber grandeur, which all the travelers felt. It was the same river that had received De Soto's body many generations before, and it was still a mystery.

"We know where it goes to, for the sea receives them all," said Mr. Pennypacker, "but no man knows whence it comes."

"And it would take a good long trip to find out," said Sol.

"A trip that we haven't time to take," returned the schoolmaster.

Henry felt a desire to make that journey, to follow the great stream, month after month, until he traced it to the last fountain and uncovered its secret. The power that grips the explorer, that draws him on through danger, known and unknown, held him as he gazed.

They followed the banks of the stream at a slow pace to the north, sweltering in the heat which seemed to come to a focus here at the confluence of great waters, until at last they reached a wide extent of low country overgrown with bushes and cut with a broad yellow band coming down from the northeast.

"The Ohio!" said Ross.

And so it was; it was here that the stream called by the Indians "The Beautiful River"--though not deserving the name at this place--lost itself in the Mississippi and at the junction it seemed full as mighty a river as the great Father of Waters himself.

They did not stay long at the meeting of the two rivers, fearing the miasma of the marshy soil, but retreated to the hills where they went into camp again. Yet Ross, and Henry, and Sol crossed both the Ohio and the Mississippi in the frail canoe for the sake of saying that they had been on the farther shores. The three, leaving Paul and the schoolmaster to guard the camp, even penetrated to a considerable distance in the prairie country beyond the Ohio. Here Henry saw for the first time a buffalo herd of size. Buffaloes were common enough in Kentucky, but the country being mostly wooded they roamed there in small bands. North of the Ohio he now beheld these huge shaggy animals in thousands and he narrowly escaped being trampled to death by a herd which, frightened by a pack of wolves, rushed down upon him like a storm. It was Ross who saved him by shooting the leading bull, thus compelling them to divide when they came to his body, by which action they left a clear space where he and Henry stood. After that Henry, as became one of fast-ripening experience and judgment, grew more cautious.

All the party were in keen enjoyment of the great journey, and felt in their veins the thrill of the wilderness. Paul's studious face took on the brown tan of autumn, and even the schoolmaster, a man of years who liked the ways of civilization, saw only the pleasures of the forest and closed his eyes to its hardships. But there was none who was caught so deeply in the spell of the wilderness as Henry, not even Ross nor the shiftless one. There was something in the spirit of the boy that responded to the call of the winds through the deep woods, a harking back to the man primeval, a love for nature and silence.

The forest hid many things from the schoolmaster, but he knew the hearts of men, and he could read their thoughts in their eyes, and he was the first to notice the change in Henry or rather less a change than a deepening and strengthening of a nature that had not found until now its true medium. The boy did not like to hear them speak of the return, he loved his people and he would serve them always as best he could, but they were prosperous and happy back there in Wareville and did not need him; now the forest beckoned to him, and, speaking to him in a hundred voices, bade him stay. When he roamed the woods, their majesty and leafy silence appealed to all his senses. The two vast still rivers threw over him the spell of mystery, and the secret of the greater one, its hidden origin, tantalized him. Often he gazed northward along its yellow current and wondered if he could not pierce that secret. Dimly in his mind, formed a plan to follow the yellow stream to its source some day, and again he thrilled with the thought of great adventures and mighty wanderings, where men of his race had never gone before.

Knowledge, too, came to him with an ease and swiftness that filled with surprise experienced foresters like Ross and Sol. The woods seemed to unfold their secrets to him. He learned the nature of all the herbs, those that might be useful to man and those that might be harmful, he was already as skillful with a canoe as either the guide or the shiftless one, he could follow a trail like an Indian, and the habits of the wild animals he observed with a minute and remembering eye. All the lore of those far-away primeval ancestors suddenly reappeared in him at the voice of the woods, and was ready for his use.

"It will not be long until Henry is a man," said Ross one evening as they sat before their camp fire and saw the boy approaching, a deer that he had killed borne upon his shoulders.

"He is a man now," said the schoolmaster with gravity and emphasis as he looked attentively at the figure of the youth carrying the deer. No one ever before had given him such an impression of strength and physical alertness. He seemed to have grown, to have expanded visibly since their departure from Wareville. The muscles of his arm stood up under the close-fitting deerskin tunic, and the length of limb and breadth of shoulder in the boy indicated a coming man of giant mold.

"What a hunter and warrior he will make!" said Ross.

"A future leader of wilderness men," said Mr. Pennypacker softly, "but there is wild blood in those veins; he will have to be handled well."

Henry threw down the deer and greeted them with cheerful words that came spontaneously from a joyful soul. They had built their fire, not a large one, in an oak opening and all around the trees rose like a mighty circular wall. The red shadows of a sun that had just set lingered on the western edge of the forest, but in the east all was black. Out of this vastness came the rustling sound of the wind as it moved among the autumn leaves. In the opening was a core of ruddy light and the living forms of men, but it was only a tiny spot in the immeasurable wilderness.

The schoolmaster and he alone felt their littleness. The autumn night was crisp, and from his seat on a log he held out his fingers to the warm blaze. Now and then a yellow or red leaf caught in the light wind drifted to his feet and he gazed up half in fear at the great encircling wall of blackness. Then he uttered silent thanks that he was with such trusty men as the guide and the shiftless one.

The effect upon Henry was not the same. He had become silent while the others talked, and he half reclined against a tree, looking at the sky that showed a dim and shadowy disk through the opening. But there was nothing of fear in his mind. A delicious sense of peace and satisfaction crept over him. All the voices of the night seemed familiar and good. A lizard slipped through the grass and the eye and ear of Henry alone noticed it; neither the guide nor the shiftless one had seen or heard its passage. He measured the disk of the heavens with his glance and foretold unerringly whether it would be clear or cloudy on the morrow, and when something rustled in the woods, he knew, without looking, that it was a hare frightened by the blaze fleeing from its covert. A tiny brook trickled at the far edge of the fire's rim, and he could tell by the color of the waters through what kind of soil it had come.

Paul sat down near him, and began to talk of home. Henry smiled upon him indulgently; his old relation of protector to the younger boy had grown stronger during this trip; in the forest he was his comrade's superior by far, and Paul willingly admitted it; in such matters he sought no rivalry with his friend.

"I wonder what they are doing way down there?" said Paul, waving his hand toward the southeast. "Just think of it, Henry! they are only one little spot in the wilderness, and we are only another little spot way up here! In all the hundreds of miles between, there may not be another white face!"

"It is likely true, but what of it?" replied Henry. "The bigger the wilderness the more room in it for us to roam in. I would rather have great forests than great towns."

He turned lazily and luxuriously on his side, and, gazing into the red coals, began to see there visions of other forests and vast plains, with himself wandering on among the trees and over the swells. His comrades said nothing more because it was comfortable in their little camp, and the peace of the wilds was over them all. The night was cold, but the circling wall of trees sheltered the opening, and the fire in the center radiated a grateful heat in which they basked. The scholar, Mr. Pennypacker, rested his face upon his hands, and he, too, was dreaming as he stared into the blaze. Paul, his blanket wrapped around him and his head pillowed upon soft boughs, was asleep already. Ross and Sol dozed.

But Henry neither slept nor wished to do so. His gaze shifted from the red coals to the silver disk of the sky. The world seemed to him very beautiful and very intimate. These illimitable expanses of forest conveyed to him no sense of either awe or fear. He was at home. He had become for the time a being of the night, piercing the darkness with the eyes of a wild creature, and hearkening to the familiar voices around him that spoke to him and to him alone. Never was sleep farther from him. The shifting firelight in its flickering play fell upon his face and revealed it in all its clear young boyish strength, the firm neck, the masterful chin, the calm, resolute eyes set wide apart, the lean big-boned fingers, lying motionless across his knees.

Mr. Pennypacker began to nod, then he, too, wrapped himself in his blanket, lay back and soon fell fast asleep; in a few minutes Sol followed him to the land of real dreams, and after a brief interval Ross, too, yielded. Henry alone was awake, drinking deep of the night and its lonely joy.

The silver disk of the sky turned into gray under a cloud, the darkness swept up deeper and thicker, the light of the fire waned, but the boy still leaned against the log, and upon his sensitive mind every change of the wilderness was registered as upon the delicate surface of a plate. He glanced at his sleeping comrades and smiled. The smile was the index to an unconscious feeling of superiority. Ross and Sol were two or three times his age, but they slept while he watched, and not Ross himself in all his years in the wilderness had learned many things that came to him by intuition.

Hours passed and the boy was yet awake. New feelings, vague and undetermined came into his mind but through them all went the feeling of mastery. He, though a boy, was in many respects the chief, and while he need not assert his leadership yet a while, he could never doubt its possession.

The light died far down and only a few smoldering coals were left. The blackness of the night, coming ever closer and closer, hovered over his companions and hid their faces from him. The great trunks of the trees grew shadowy and dim. Out of the darkness came a sound slight but not in harmony with the ordinary noises of the forest. His acute senses, the old inherited primitive instinct, noticed at once the jarring note. He moved ever so little but an extraordinary change came over his face. The idle look of luxury and basking warmth passed away and the eyes became alert, watchful, defiant. Every feature, every muscle was drawn, as if he were at the utmost tension. Almost unconsciously his figure sank down farther against the log, until it blended perfectly with the bark and the fallen leaves below. Only an eye of preternatural keenness could have separated the outline of the boy from the general scene.

For five minutes he lay and moved not a particle. Then the discordant note came again among the familiar sounds of the forest and he glanced at his comrades. They slept peacefully. His lip curled slightly, not with contempt but with that unconscious feeling of superiority; they would not have noticed, even had they been awake.

His hands moved forward and grasped his rifle. Then he began to slip away from the opening and into the forest, not by walking nor altogether by crawling, but by a curious, noiseless, gliding motion, almost like that of a serpent. Always he clung to the shadows where his shifting body still blended with the dark, and as he advanced other primitive instincts blazed up in him. He was a hunter pursuing for the first time the highest and most dangerous game of all game and the thrill through his veins was so keen that he shivered slightly. His chin was projected, and his eyes were two red spots in the night. All the while his comrades by the fire, even the trained foresters, slumbered in peace, no warning whatever coming to their heavy heads.

The boy reached the wall of the woods, and now his form was completely swallowed up in the blackness there. He lay a while in the bushes, motionless, all his senses alert, and for the third time the jarring note came to his ears. The maker of it was on his right, and, as he judged, perhaps a couple of hundred yards away. He would proceed at once to that point. It is truth to say that no thought of danger entered his mind; the thrills of the present and its chances absorbed him. It seemed natural that he should do this thing, he was merely resuming an old labor, discontinued for a time.

He raised his head slightly, but even his keen eyes could see nothing in the forest save trunks and branches, ghostly and shapeless, and the regular rustle of the wind was not broken now by the jarring note. But the darkness heavy and ominous, was permeated with the signs of things about to happen, and heavy with danger, a danger, however, that brought no fear to Henry for himself, only for others. A faint sighing note as of a distant bird came on the wind, and pausing, he listened intently. He knew that it was not a bird, that sound was made by human lips, and once more a light shiver passed over his frame; it was a signal, concerning his comrades and himself, and he would turn aside the danger from those old friends of his who slept by the fire, in peace and unknowing.

He resumed his cautious passage through the undergrowth, and, the inherited instinct blossoming so suddenly into full flower, was still his guide. Not a sound marked his advance, the forest fell silently behind him, and he went on with unerring knowledge to the spot from which the discordant sounds had come.

He approached another opening among the trees, like unto that in which his comrades slept, and now, lying close in the undergrowth, he looked for the first time upon the sight which so often boded ill to his kind. The warriors were in a group, some sitting others standing, and though there was no fire and the moonlight was slight he could mark the primitive brutality of their features, the nature of the animal that fought at all times for life showing in their eyes. They were hard, harsh and repellent in every aspect, but the boy felt for a moment a singular attraction, there was even a distant feeling of kinship as if he, too, could live this life and had lived it. But the feeling quickly passed, and in its place came the thought of his comrades whom he must save.

The older of the warriors talked in a low voice, saying unknown words in a harsh, guttural tongue, and Henry could guess only at their meaning. But they seemed to be awaiting a signal and presently the low thrilling note was heard again. Then the warriors turned as if this were the command to do so, and came directly toward the boy who lay in the darkest shadows of the undergrowth.

Henry was surprised and startled but only for a moment, then the primeval instinct came to his aid and swiftly he sank away in the bushes in front of them, as before, no sound marking his passage. He thought rapidly and in all his thoughts there was none of himself but as the savior of the little party. It seemed to come to him naturally that he should be the protector and champion.

When he had gone about fifty yards he uttered a shout, long, swelling and full of warning. Then he turned to his right and crashed through the undergrowth, purposely making a noise that the pursuing warriors could not fail to hear. Ross and the others, he knew, would be aroused instantly by his cry and would take measures of safety. Now the savages would be likely to follow him alone, and he noted by the sounds that they had turned aside to do so.

At this moment Henry Ware felt nothing but exultation that he, a boy, should prove himself a match for all the cunning of the forest-bred, and he thought not at all of the pursuit that came so fiercely behind him.

He ran swiftly and now directly more than a mile from the camp of his friends. Then the inherited instinct that had served him so well failed; it could not warn him of the deep little river that lay straight across his path flowing toward the Mississippi. He came out upon its banks and was ready to drop down in its waters, but he saw that before he could reach the farther shore he would be a target for his pursuers. He hesitated and was about to turn at a sharp angle, but the warriors emerged from the forest. It was then too late.

The savages uttered a shout of triumph, the long, ferocious, whining note, so terrible in its intensity and meaning, and Henry, raising his rifle, fired at a painted breast. The next moment they were hurled upon him in a brown mass. He felt a stunning blow upon the head, sparks flew before his eyes, and the world reeled away into darkness.

CHAPTER XII
THE PRIMITIVE MAN

WHEN Henry came back to his world he was lying upon the ground, with his head against a log, and about him was a circle of brown faces, cold, hard, expressionless and apparently devoid of human feeling; pity and mercy seemed to be unknown qualities there. But the boy met them with a gaze as steady as their own, and then he glanced quickly around the circle. There was no other prisoner and he saw no ghastly trophy; then his comrades had escaped, and, deep satisfaction in his heart, he let his head fall back upon the log. They could do now as they chose with him, and whatever it might be he felt that he had no cause to fear it.

Three other warriors came in presently, and Henry judged that all the party were now gathered there. He was still lying near the river on whose banks he had been struck down, and the shifting clouds let the moonlight fall upon him. He put his hand to his head where it ached, and when he took it away, there was blood on his fingers. He inferred that a heavy blow had been dealt to him with the flat of a tomahawk, but with the stained fingers he made a scornful gesture. One of the warriors, apparently a chief, noticed the movement, and he muttered a word or two which seemed to have the note of approval. Henry rose to his feet and the chief still regarded him, noting the fearless look, and the hint of surpassing physical powers soon to come. He put his hand upon the boy's shoulder and pointed toward the north and west. Henry understood him. His life was to be spared for the present, at least, and he was to go with them into the northwest, but to what fate he knew not.

One of the warriors bathed his head, and put upon it a lotion of leaves which quickly drove away the pain. Henry suffered his ministrations with primitive stoicism, making no comment and showing no interest.

At a word from the leader they took up their silent march, skirting the river for a while until they came to a shallow place, where they forded it, and buried themselves again in the dark forest. They passed among its shades swiftly, silently and in single file, Henry near the middle of the column, his figure in the dusk blending into the brown of theirs. He had completely recovered his strength, and, save for the separation from his friends and their consequent wonder and sorrow, he would not have grieved over the mischance. Instinct told him--perhaps it was his youth, perhaps his ready adaptability that appealed to his captors--that his life was safe--and now he felt a keen curiosity to know the outcome. It seemed to him too that without any will of his own he was about to begin the vast wanderings that he had coveted.

Hour after hour the silent file trod swiftly on into the northwest, no one speaking, their footfalls making no sound on the soft earth. The moonlight deepened again, and veiled the trunks and branches in ghostly silver or gray. By and by it grew darker and then out of the blackness came the first shoot of dawn. A shaft of pale light appeared in the east, then broadened and deepened, bringing in its trail, in terrace after terrace, the red and gold of the rising sun. Then the light swept across the heavens and it was full day.

They were yet in the forest and the dawn was cold. Here and there in the open spaces and on the edges of the brown leaves appeared the white gleam of frost. The rustle of the woods before the western wind was chilly in the ear. But Henry was without sign of fatigue or cold. He walked with a step as easy and as tireless as that of the strongest warrior in the band, and at all times he held himself, as if he were one of them, not their prisoner.

About an hour after dawn the party which numbered fifteen men halted at a signal from the chief and began to eat the dried meat of the buffalo, taken from their pouches. They gave him a good supply of the food, and he found it tough but savory. Hunger would have given a sufficient sauce to anything and as he ate in a sort of luxurious content he studied his captors with the advantage of the daylight. The full sunshine disclosed no more of softness and mercy than the night had shown. The features were immobile, the eyes fixed and hard, but when the gaze of any one of them, even the chief, met the boy's it was quickly turned. There was about them something furtive, something of the lower kingdom of the animals. That inherited primitive instinct, recently flaming up with such strength in him, did not tell him that they were his full brethren. But he did not hate them, instead they interested him.

After eating they rested an hour or more in the covert of a thicket and Henry saw the beautiful day unfold. The sunshine was dazzling in its glory, the crisp wind made one's blood sparkle like a tonic, and it was good merely to live. A vast horizon inclosed only the peace of the wilderness.

The chief said some words to Henry, but the boy could understand none of them, and he shook his head. Then the chief took the rifle that had belonged to the captive, tapped it on the barrel and pointed toward the southeast. Henry nodded to indicate that he had come from that point, and then smiling swept the circle of the northwestern horizon with his hands. He meant to say that he would go with them without resistance, for the present, at least, and the chief seemed to understand, as his face relaxed into a look of comprehension and even of good nature.

Their march was resumed presently and as before it was straight into the northwest. They passed out of the forest crossed the Ohio in hidden canoes and entered a region of small but beautiful prairies, cut by shallow streams, which they waded with undiminished speed. Henry began to suspect that the band came from some very distant country, and was hastening so much in order not to be caught on the hunting grounds of rival tribes. The northwesterly direction that they were following confirmed him in this belief.

All the day passed on the march but shortly after the night came on and they had eaten a little more of the jerked meat, they lay down in a thicket, and Henry, unmindful of his captivity, fell in a few minutes into a sleep that was deep, sweet and dreamless. He did not know then that before he was asleep long the chief took a robe of tanned deerskin and threw it over him, shielding his body from the chill autumn night. In the morning shortly before he awoke the chief took away the robe.

That day they came to a mighty river and Henry knew that the yellow stream was that of the Mississippi. The Indians dragged from the sheltering undergrowth two canoes, in which the whole party paddled up stream until nightfall, when they hid the canoes again in the foliage on the western shore, and then encamped on the crest. They seemed to feel that they were out of danger now as they built a fine fire and the captive basked in its warmth.

Henry had not made the slightest effort to escape, nor had he indicated any wish to do so, finding his reward in the increased freedom which the warriors gave to him. He had never been bound and now he could walk as he chose in a limited area about the camp. But he did not avail himself of the privilege, for the present, preferring to sit by the fire, where he saw pictures of Wareville and those whom he loved. Then he had a swift twinge of conscience. When they heard they would grieve deep and long for him and one, his mother, would never forget. He should have sought more eagerly to escape, and he glanced quickly about him, but there was no chance. However careless the warriors might seem there was always one between him and the forest. He resigned himself with a sigh but had he thought how quickly the pain passed his conscience would have hurt him again. Now he felt much comfort where he sat; the night was really cold, bitingly cold, and it was a glorious fire. As he sat before it and basked in its radiance he felt the glorious physical joy that must have thrilled some far-away primeval ancestor, as he hugged the coals in his cave after coming in from the winter storm.

Henry had the best place by the fire and a warrior who was sitting where his back was exposed to the wind moved over and shoved him away. Henry without a word smote him in the face with such force that the man fell flat and Henry thrust him aside, resuming his original position. The warrior rose to his feet and rubbed his bruised face, looking doubtfully at the boy who sat in such stolid silence, staring into the coals and paying no further attention to his opponent. The Indian never uses his fists, and his hand strayed to the handle of his tomahawk; then, as it strayed away again he sat down on the far side of the fire, and he too began to stare stolidly into the red coals. The chief, Black Cloud, bestowed on both a look of approval, but uttered no comment.

Presently Black Cloud gave some orders to his men and they lay down to sleep, but the chief took the deerskin robe and handed it to

Henry. His manner was that of one making a gift, and a gesture confirmed the impression. Henry took the robe which he would need and thanked the chief in words whose meaning the donor might gather from the tone. Then he lay down and slept as before a dreamless sleep all through the night.

Their journey lasted many days and every hour of it was full of interest to Henry, appealing alike to his curiosity and its gratification. He was launched upon the great wandering and he found in it both the glamour and the reality that he wished, the reality in the rivers and the forests and the prairies that he saw, and the glamour in the hope of other and greater rivers and forests and prairies to come.

Indian summer was at hand. All the woods were dyed in vivid colors, reds and yellows and browns, and glowed with dazzling hues in the intense sunlight. Often the haze of Indian summer hung afar and softened every outline. Henry's feeling that he was one of the band grew stronger, and they, too, began to regard him as their own. His freedom was extended more and more and with astonishing quickness he soon picked up enough words of their dialect to make himself intelligible. They took him with them, when they turned aside for hunting expeditions, and he was permitted now and then to use his own rifle. Only six men in the band had guns, and two of these guns were rifles the other four being muskets. Henry soon showed that he was the best marksman among them and respect for him grew. The Indian whom he knocked down was slightly gored by a stag when only Henry was near, but Henry slew the stag, bound up the man's wound and stayed by him until the others came. The warrior, Gray Fox, speedily became one of his best friends.

Henry's enjoyment became more intense; all the trammels of civilization were now thrown aside, he never thought of the morrow because the day with its interests was sufficient, and from his new friends he learned fresh lore of the forest with marvelous rapidity; they taught him how to trail, to take advantage of every shred of cover and to make signals by imitating the cry of bird or beast. Once they were caught in a hailstorm, when it turned bitterly cold, but he endured it as well as the best of them, and made not a single complaint.

They came at last to their village, a great distance west of the Mississippi, a hundred lodges perhaps, pitched in a warm and sheltered valley and the boy, under the fostering care of Black Cloud, was formally adopted into the tribe, taking up at once the thread of his new life, and finding in it the same keen interest that had marked all the stages of the great journey.

The climate here was colder than that from which he had come, and winter, with fierce winds from the Great Plains was soon upon them. But the camp which was to remain there until spring was well chosen and the steep hills about them fended off the worst of the blast. Yet the snow came soon in great, whirling flakes and fell all one night. The next morning the boy saw the world in white and he found it singularly beautiful. The snow he did not mind as clothing of dressed skins had been given to him and he had a warm buffalo robe for a blanket. Now, young as he was, he became one of the best hunters for the village and with the others he roamed far over the snowy hills in search of game. Many were the prizes that fell to his steady aim and eye, chief among them the deer, the bear and the buffalo.

His fame in the village grew fast, and it would be hiding the fact to deny that he enjoyed it. The wild rough life with its limitless range over time and space appealed to every instinct in him, and his new fame as a tireless and skillful hunter was very sweet to him. He thought of his people and Wareville, it is true, but he consoled himself again with the belief that they were well and he would return to them when the chance came, and then he plunged all the deeper and with all the more zest into his new life which had so many fascinations. At Wareville there were certain bounds which he must respect, certain weights which he must carry, but here he was free from both.

Meanwhile his body thrived at a prodigious rate. One could almost see him grow. There was not a warrior in the village who was as strong as he, and already he surpassed them all in endurance; none was so fleet of foot nor so tireless. His face and hair darkened in the wind and sun, his last vestige of civilized garb had disappeared long ago, and he was clothed wholly in deerskin. His features grew stronger and keener and the eyes were incessantly watchful, roving hither and thither, covering every point within range. It would have taken more than a casual glance now to discover that he was white.

The winter deepened. The snow was continuous, fierce blasts blew in from the distant western plains and even searched out their sheltered valley. The old men and the women shivered in the lodges, but sparkling young blood and tireless action kept the boy warm and flourishing through it all. Game grew scarce about them and the hunters went far westward in search of the buffalo.

Henry was with the party that traveled farthest toward the setting sun, and it was long before they returned. Winter was at its height and when they came out of the forest into the waving open stretches which are the Great Plains all things were hidden by the snow.

Henry from the summit of a little hill saw before him an expanse as mighty as the sea, and like it in many of its aspects. They told him that it rolled away to the westward, no man knew how far, as none of them had ever come to the end of it. In summer it was covered with life. Here grew thick grass and wild flowers and the buffalo passed in millions.

It inspired in Henry a certain awe and yet by its very vagueness and immensity it attracted. Just as he had wished to explore the secrets of the forest he would like now to tread the Great Plains and find what they held.

They turned toward the southwest in search of buffalo and were caught in a great storm of wind and hail. The cold was bitter and the wind cut to the bone. They were saved from freezing to death only by digging a rude shelter through the snow into the side of a hill, and there they crouched for two days with so little food left in their knapsacks, that without game, they would perish, in a week, of hunger, if the cold did not get the first chance. The most experienced hunters went forth, but returned with nothing, thankful for so little a mercy as the ability to get back to their half-shelter.

Henry at last took his rifle and ventured out alone--the others were too listless to stop him--and before the noon hour he found a buffalo bull, some outcast from the herd which had gone southward, struggling in the snow. The bull was old and lean, and it took two bullets to bring him down, but his death meant their life and Henry hurried to the camp with the joyful news. It was clearly recognized that he had saved them, but no one said anything and Henry was glad of their silence.

When the storm ceased they renewed their journey toward the south with a plentiful supply of food and not long afterwards the snow began to melt. Under the influence of a warm wind out of the southwest it disappeared with marvelous quickness; one day the earth was all white, and the next it was all brown. The warm wind continued to blow, and then faint touches of green began to appear in the dead grass; there were delicate odors, the breath of the great warm south, and they knew that spring was not far away.

In a week they ran into the buffalo herd, a mighty black mass of moving millions. The earth rumbled hollowly under the tread of a myriad feet, and the plain was black with bodies to the horizon and beyond.

They killed as many of the buffalo as they wished and after the fashion of the more northerly Indians reduced the meat to pemmican. Then, each man bearing as much as he could conveniently carry, they began their swift journey homeward, not knowing whether they would arrive in time for the needs of the village.

Henry felt a deep concern for these new friends of his who were left behind in the valley. He shared the anxiety of the others who feared lest they would be too late and that fact reconciled him to the retreat from the Great Plains, whose mysteries he longed to unravel.

As they went swiftly eastward the spring unfolded so fast that it seemed to Henry to come with one great jump. They were now in the forests and everywhere the trees were laden with fresh buds, in all the open spaces the young grass was springing up, and the brooks, as if rejoicing in their new freedom from the ice-bound winter, ran in sparkling little streams between green banks.

The physical world was full of beauty to him, more so than ever because his power of feeling it had grown. During the winter and by the triumphant endurance of so many hardships his form had expanded and the tide of sparkling blood had risen higher. Although a captive he was regarded in a sense as the leader of the hunting party; it was obvious, in the deference that the others, though much older, showed to him and he knew that only his resource, courage and endurance had saved them all from death. A song of triumph was singing in his veins.

They found the village at the edge of starvation despite the approach of spring; two or three of the older people had died already of weakness, and their supplies arrived just in time to relieve the crisis. There were willing tongues to tell of his exploits, and Henry soon perceived that he was a hero to them all and he enjoyed it, because it was natural to him to be a leader, and he loved to breathe the air of approbation. Yet as they valued him more they grew more jealous of him, and they watched him incessantly, lest he should take it into his head to flee to the people who were once his own. Henry saw the difficulty and again it soothed his conscience by showing to him that he could not do what he yet had a lingering feeling that he ought to do.

Good luck seemed to come in a shower to the village with the return of the hunting party. Spring leaped suddenly into full bloom, and the woods began to swarm with game. It was the most plentiful season that the oldest man could recall, there was no hunter so lazy and so dull that he could not find the buffalo and the deer.

Then the band, with the spirit of irresponsible wandering upon it, took down its lodges and traveled slowly into the north farther and farther from the little settlement away down in Kentucky. There was peace among the tribes and they could go as they chose. They came at last to the shores of a mighty lake, Superior, and here when Henry looked out upon an expanse of water, as limitless to the eyes as the sea, he felt the same thrill of awe that had passed through his veins when the Great Plains lay outspread before him. As it was now midsummer and the forests crackled in the heat they lingered long by the deep cool waters of the lake. Here white traders, Frenchmen speaking a tongue unknown to Henry, came to them with rifles, ammunition and bright-colored blankets to trade for furs. More than one of them saw and admired the tall powerful young warrior with the singularly watchful eyes but not one of them knew that under his paint and tan he was whiter than themselves; instead they took him to be the wildest of the wild.

Henry's heart had throbbed a little at the first sight of them, but it was only for a moment, then it beat as steadily as ever; white like himself they might be, but they were of an alien race; their speech was not his speech, their ways not his ways and he turned from them. He was glad when they were gone.

Toward the end of summer they went south again and wandered idly through pleasant places. It was still a full season with wild fruits hanging from the trees and game everywhere. There had been no sickness in the little tribe and they basked in physical content. It was now a careless easy life with the stimulus of wandering and hunting and all the old primeval instincts in Henry, made stronger by habit, were gratified. He fell easily into the ways of his friends; when there was nothing to do he could sit for hours looking at the forests and the streams and the sunshine, letting his soul steep in the glory of it all. To his other qualities he now added that of illimitable patience. He could wait for what he wished as the Eskimo sits for days at the air hole until the seal appears.

In their devious wanderings they kept a general course toward the valley in which they had passed the first winter, intending to renew their camp there during the cold weather, but autumn, as they intended, was at hand before they reached it. They were yet a long distance north and west of their valley when they were threatened by a danger with which they had not reckoned. A local tribe claimed that the band was infringing upon their hunting grounds and began war with a treacherous attack upon a hunting party.

The war was not long but the few hundreds who took part in it shared all the passions and fierce emotions of two great nations in conflict. Henry was in the thick of it, first alike in attack and defense, superior to the Indians themselves in wiles and cunning. Several of the hostile tribe fell at his hand, although he could not take a scalp, the remnants of his early training forbidding it. But once or twice he was ashamed of the weakness. The hostile party was triumphantly beaten off with great loss to itself and Henry and his friends pursued their journey leisurely and triumphantly. Now besides being a great hunter he was a great warrior too.

CHAPTER XIII
THE CALL OF DUTY

THEY arrived at their valley and prepared for the second winter there, returning to the place for several reasons, chief among them being the right of prescription, to which the other tribes yielded tacit consent. The Indian recks little of the future, but in his reversion to primitive type Henry had taken with him much of the acquired and modern knowledge of education. He looked ahead, and, under his constant suggestion, advice and pressure they stored so much food for the winter that there was no chance of another famine, whatever might happen to the game.

Before they went into winter quarters Henry clearly perceived one thing--he was first in the little tribe; even Black Cloud, the chief, willingly took second place to him. He was first alike in strength and wisdom and it was patent to all. He was now, although only a boy in years, nearly at his full height, almost a head above an ordinary warrior, with wonderfully keen eyes, set wide apart, and a square projecting chin, so firm that it seemed to be carved of brown marble. His shoulders were of great breadth, but his lean figure had all the graceful strength and ease of some wild animal native to the forest. He was scrupulous in his attire, and wore only the finest skins and furs that the village could furnish.

Henry felt the deference of the tribe and it pleased him. He glided naturally into the place of leader, feeling the responsibility and liking it. He was tactful, too, he would not push Black Cloud from his old position, but merely remained at his right hand and ruled through him. The chief was soothed and flattered, and the arrangement worked to the pleasure of both, and to the great good of the village which now enjoyed a winter of prosperity hitherto unknown to such natives of the woods. Nobody had to go hungry, there was abundant provision against the cold. Henry, though not saying it, knew that with him the credit lay, and just now the world seemed very full. As human beings go he was thoroughly happy; the life fitted him, satisfied all his wants, and the memory of his own people became paler and more distant; they could do very well without him; they were so many, one could be spared, and when the chance came he would send word to them that he was alive and well, but that he would not come back.

When the buds began to burst they traveled eastward, until they came to the Mississippi. The sight of its stream brought back to Henry a thought of those with whom he had first seen it and he felt a pang of remorse. But the pang was fleeting, and the memory too he resolutely put aside.

They crossed the Mississippi and advanced into the land of little prairies, a green, rich region, pleasant to the eye and full of game. They wandered and hunted here, drifting slowly to the eastward, until they came upon a great encampment of the fierce and warlike nation, known as the Shawnees. The Shawnees were in their war paint and were singing warlike songs. It was evident to the most casual visitor that they were going forth to do battle.

It was late in the afternoon when Henry, Black Cloud and two others came upon this encampment. His own band had pitched its lodges some miles behind, but the kinship of the forest and the peace between them, made the four the guests of the Shawnees as long as they chose to stay.

At least a thousand warriors were in all the hideous varieties of war paint, and the scene, in the waning light, was weird and ominous even to Henry. The war songs in their very monotony were chilling, and full of ferocity, and in all the thousand faces there was not one that shone with the light of kindness and mercy.

Long glances were cast at Henry, but even their keen eyes failed to notice that he was not an Indian, and he stood watching them, his face impassive, but his interest aroused. A dozen warriors naked to the waist and hideously painted were singing a war song, while they capered and jumped to its unrhythmic tune. Suddenly one of them snatched something from his girdle and waved it aloft in triumph. Henry knew that it was a scalp, many of which he had seen, and he paid little attention, but the Indian came closer, still singing and dancing, and waving his hideous trophy.

The scalp flashed before Henry's eyes, and it displayed not the coarse black locks of the savage, but hair long, fine and yellow like silk. He knew that it was the scalp of a white girl, and a sudden, shuddering horror seized him. It had belonged to one of his own kind, to the race into which he had been born and with which he had passed his boyhood. His heart filled with hatred of these Shawnees, but the warriors of his own little tribe would take scalps, and if occasion came, the scalps of white people, yes, of white women and white girls! He tried to dismiss the thought or rather to crush it down, but it would not yield to his will; always it rose up again.

He walked back to the edge of the encampment, where some of the warriors were yet singing the war songs that with all of their monotony were so weird and chilling. Twilight was over the forest, save in the west, where a blood-red tint from the sunken sun lingered on trunk and bough, and gleamed across the faces of the dancing warriors. In this lurid light Henry suddenly saw them savage, inhuman, implacable. They were truly creatures of the wilderness, the lust of blood was upon them, and they would shed it for the pleasure of seeing it flow. Henry's primeval world darkened as he looked upon them.

He was about to leave with Black Cloud and his friends when it occurred to him to ask which way the war party was going and who were the destined victims. He spoke to two or three warriors until he came to one who understood the tongue of his little tribe.

The man waved his hand toward the south.

"Off there; far away," he said. "Beyond the great river."

Henry knew that in this case "great river" meant the Ohio and he was somewhat surprised; it was still a long journey from the Ohio to the land of the Cherokees, Chickasaws and Choctaws with whom the Northern tribes sometimes fought, and he spoke of it to the warrior, but the man shook his head, and said they were going against the white people; there was a village of them in a sheltered valley beside a little river, they had been there three or four years and had flourished in peace; freedom so long from danger had made them careless, but the Shawnee scouts had looked from the woods upon the settlement, and the war band would slay or take them all with ease.

The man had not spoken a half dozen words before Henry knew that Wareville was the place, upon which the doom was so soon to fall. The chill of horror that had seized him at sight of the yellow-haired scalp passed over him again, deeper, stronger and longer than before. And the colony would fall! There could be no doubt of it! Nothing could save it! The hideous band, raging with tomahawk and knife, would dash without a word of warning, like a bolt from the sky upon Wareville so long sheltered and peaceful in its valley. And he could see all the phases of the savage triumph, the surprise, the triumphant and ferocious yells, the rapid volleys of the rifles, the flashing of the blades, the burning buildings, the shouts, the cries, and men, women and children in one red slaughter. In another year the forest would be springing up where Wareville had been, and the wolf and the fox would prowl among the charred timbers. And among the bleaching bones would be those of his own mother and sister and Lucy Upton--if they were not taken away for a worse fate.

He endured the keenest thrill of agony that life had yet held for him. All his old life, the dear familiar ties surged up, and were hot upon his brain. His place was there! with them! not here! He had yielded too easily to the spell of the woods and the call of the old primeval nature. He might have escaped long ago, there had been many opportunities, but he could not see them. His blindness had been willful, the child of his own desires. He knew it too well now. He saw himself guilty and guilty he was.

But in that moment of agony and fear for his own he was paying the price of his guilt. The sense of helplessness was crushing. In two hours the war party would start and it would flit southward like the wind, as silent but far more deadly. No, nothing could save the innocent people at Wareville; they were as surely doomed as if their destruction had already taken place.

But not one of these emotions, so tense and so deep, was written on the face of him whom even the Shawnees did not know to be white. Not a feature changed, the Indian stoicism and calm, the product alike of his nature and cultivation, clung to him. His eyes were veiled and his movements had their habitual gravity and dignity.

He walked with Black Cloud to the edge of the encampment, said farewell to the Shawnees, and then, with a great surge of joy, his resolution came to him. It was so sudden, so transforming that the whole world changed at once. The blood-red tint, thrown by the sunken sun, was gone from the forest, but instead the silver sickle of the moon was rising and shed a radiant light of hope.

He said nothing until they had gone a mile or so and then, drawing Black Cloud aside, spoke to him words full of firmness, but not without feeling. He made no secret of his purpose, and he said that if Black Cloud and the others sought to stay him with force with force he would reply. He must go, and he would go at once.

Black Cloud was silent for a while, and Henry saw the faintest quiver in his eyes. He knew that he held a certain place in the affections of the chief, not the place that he might hold in the regard of a white man, it was more limited and qualified, but it was there, nevertheless.

"I am the captive of the tribe I know," said Henry. "It has made me its son, but my white blood is not changed and I must save my people. The Shawnees march south to-night against them and I go to give warning. It is better that I go in peace."

He spoke simply, but with dignity, and looked straight into the eyes of the chief, where he saw that slight pathetic quiver come again.

"I cannot keep you now if you would go," said Black Cloud, "but it may be when you are far away that the forest and we with whom you have lived and hunted so many seasons will call to you again, in a voice to which you must listen."

Henry was moved; perhaps the chief was telling the truth. He saw the hardships and bareness of the wilderness but the life there appealed to him and satisfied the stronger wants of his nature; he seemed to be the reincarnation of some old forest dweller, belonging to a time thousands of years ago, yet the voice of duty, which was in this case also the voice of love, called to him, too, and now with the louder voice. He would go, and there must be no delay in his going.

"Farewell, Black Cloud," he said with the same simplicity. "I will think often of you who have been good to me."

The chief called the other warriors and told them their comrade was going far to the south, and they might never see him again. Their faces expressed nothing, whatever they may have felt. Henry repeated the farewell, hesitated no longer and plunged into the forest. But he stopped when he was thirty or forty yards away and looked back. The chief and the warriors stood side by side as he had left them, motionless and gazing after him. It was night now and to eyes less keen than Henry's their forms would have melted into the dusk, but he saw every outline distinctly, the lean brown features and the black shining eyes. He waved his hands to them--a white man's action--and resumed his flight, not looking back again.

It was a dark night and the forest stretched on, black and endless, the trunks of the trees standing in rows like phantoms of the dusk. Henry looked up at the moon and the few stars, and reckoned his course. Wareville lay many hundred miles away, chiefly to the south, and he had a general idea of the direction, but the war party would know exactly, and its advantage there would perhaps be compensation for the superior speed of one man. But Henry, for the present, would not think of such a disaster as failure; on the contrary he reckoned with nothing but success, and he felt a marvelous elation.

The decision once taken the rebound had come with great force, and he felt that he was now about to make atonement for his long neglect, and more than neglect. Perhaps it had been ordained long ago that he should be there at the critical moment, see the danger and bring them the warning that would save. There was consolation in the thought.

He increased his pace and sped southward in the easy trot that he had learned from his red friends, a gait that he could maintain indefinitely, and with which he could put ground behind him at a remarkable rate. His rifle he carried at the trail, his head was bent slightly forward, and he listened intently to every sound of the forest as he passed; nothing escaped his ear, whether it was a raccoon stirring among the branches, a deer startled from its covert, or merely the wind rustling the leaves. Instinct also told him that the forest was at peace.

To the ordinary man the night with its dusk, the wilderness with its ghostly tree trunks, and the silence would have been full of weirdness and awe, black with omens and presages. Few would not have chilled to the marrow to be alone there, but to Henry it brought only hope and the thrill of exultation. He had no sense of loneliness, the forest hid no secrets for him; this was home and he merely passed through it on a great quest.

He looked up at the moon and stars, and confirmed himself in his course, though he never slackened speed as he looked. He came out of the forest upon a prairie, and here the moonlight was brighter, touching the crests of the swells with silver spear-points. A dozen buffaloes rose up and snorted as he flitted by, but he scarcely bestowed a passing glance upon the black bulk of the animals. The prairie was only two or three miles across, and at the far edge flowed a shallow creek which he crossed at full speed, and entered the forest again. Now he came to rough country, steep little hills, and a dense undergrowth of interlacing bushes, and twining thorny vines. But he made his way through them in a manner that only one forest-bred could compass, and pressed on with speed but little slackened.

When the night became darkest, in the forest just before morning he lay down in the deepest shadow of a thicket, his hand upon his rifle, and in a few minutes was sleeping soundly. It was a matter of training with him to sleep whenever sleep was needed and he had no nerves. He knew, too, despite his haste that he must save his strength, and he did not hesitate to follow the counsels of prudence.

It was his will that he should sleep about four hours, and, his system obeying the wish, he awoke at the appointed time. The sun was rising over the vast, green wilderness, lighting up a world seemingly as lonely and deserted as it had been the night before. The unbroken forest, touched with the tender tints of young spring and bathed in the pure light of the first dawn, bent gently to a west wind that breathed only of peace.

Henry stood up and inhaled the odorous air. He was a striking figure, yet a few yards away he would have been visible only to the trained eye; his half-savage garb of tanned deerskin, stained green and trimmed at the edges with green beads and little green feathers, blended with the colors of the forest and merely made a harmonious note in the whole. His figure compact, powerful and always poised as if ready for a spring swayed slightly, while his eyes that missed nothing searched every nook in the circling woods. He was then neither the savage nor the civilized man, but he had many of the qualities of both.

The slight swaying motion of his body ceased suddenly and he remained as still as a rock. He seemed to be a part of the green bushes that grew around him, yet he was never more watchful, never more alert. The indefinable sixth sense, developed in him by the wilderness, had taken alarm; there was a presence in the forest, foreign in its nature; it was not sight nor hearing nor yet smell that told him so, but a feeling or rather a sort of prescience. Then an extraordinary thrill ran through him; it was an emotion partaking in its nature of joy and anticipation; he was about to be confronted by some danger, perhaps a crisis, and the physical faculties, handed down by a far-off ancestor, expanded to meet it. He knew that he would conquer, and he felt already the glow of triumph.

Presently he sank down in the undergrowth so gently that not a bush rustled; there was no displacement of nature, the grass and the foliage were just as they had been, but the figure, visible before to the trained eye at a dozen paces, could not have been seen now at all. Then he began to creep through the grass with a swift easy gliding motion like that of a serpent, moving at a speed remarkable in such a position and quite soundless. He went a full half mile before he stopped and rose to his knees, and then his face was hidden by the bushes, although the eyes still searched every part of the forest.

His look was now wholly changed. He might be the hunted, but he bore himself as the hunter. All vestige of the civilized man, trained to humanity and mercy, was gone. Those who wished to kill were seeking him and he would kill in return. The thin lips were slightly drawn back, showing the line of white teeth, the eyes were narrowed and in them was the cold glitter of expected conflict. Brown hands, lean but big-boned and powerful, clasped a rifle having a long slender barrel and a beautifully carved stock. It was a figure, terrible alike in its manifestation of physical power and readiness, and in the fierce eye that told what quality of mind lay behind it.

He sank down again and moved in a small circle to the right. His original thrill of joy was now a permanent emotion; he was like some one playing an exciting game into which no thought of danger entered. He stopped behind a large tree, and sheltering himself riveted his eyes on a spot in the forest about fifty yards away. No one else could have found there anything suspicious, anything to tell of an alien presence, but he no longer doubted.

At the detected point a leaf moved, but not in the way it should have swayed before the gentle wind, and there was a passing spot of brown in the green of the bushes. It was visible only for a moment, but it was sufficient for the attuned mind and body of Henry Ware. Every part of him responded to the call. The rifle sprang to his shoulder and before the passing spot of brown was gone, a stream of fire spurted from its slender muzzle, and its sharp cracking report like the lashing of a whip was blended with the long-drawn howl, so terrible in its note, that is the death cry of a savage.

The bullet had scarcely left his gun before he fell back almost flat, and the answering shot sped over his head. It was for this that he sank down, and before the second shot died he sprang to his feet and rushed forward, drawing his tomahawk and uttering a shout that rolled away in fierce echoes through the forest.

He knew that his enemies were but two; in his eccentric course through the forest he had passed directly over their trail, and he had read the signs with an infallible eye. Now one was dead and the other like himself had an unloaded gun. The rest of his deed would be a mere matter of detail.

The second savage uttered his war cry and sprang forward from the bushes. He might well have recoiled at the terrible figure that rushed to meet him; in all his wild life of risks he had never before been confronted by anything so instinct with terror, so ominous of death. But he did not have time to take thought before he was overwhelmed by his resistless enemy.

It was an affair of but a few moments. The Indian threw his tomahawk but Henry parried the blade upon the barrel of his rifle which he still carried in his left hand, and his own tomahawk was whirled in a glittering curve about his head. Now it was launched with mighty force and the savage, cloven to the chin, sank soundless to the earth; he had been smitten down by a force so sudden and absolute that he died instantly.

The victor, elate though he was, paused, and quickly reloaded his rifle--wilderness caution would allow nothing else--and afterwards advancing looked first at the savage whom he had slain in the open and then at the other in the bushes. There was no pity in him, his only emotion was a great sense of power; they had hunted him, two to one, and they born in the woods, but he had outwitted and slain them both. He could have escaped, he could have easily left them far behind when he first discovered that they were stalking him, but he had felt that they should be punished and now the event justified his faith.

It was not his first taking of human life, and while he would have shuddered at the deed a year ago he felt no such sensation now; they were merely dangerous wild animals that had crossed his path, and he had put them out of it in the proper way; his feeling was that of the hunter who slays a grizzly bear or a lion, only he had slain two.

He stood looking at them, and save for the rustling of the young grass under the gentle western wind the wilderness was silent and at peace. The sun was shooting up higher and higher and a vast golden light hung over the forest, gilding every leaf and twig. Henry Ware turned at last and sped swiftly and silently to the south, still thrilling with exultation over his deed, and the sequel that he knew would quickly come. But in the few brief minutes his nature had reverted another and further step toward the primitive.

When he had gone a half mile in his noiseless flight he stopped, and, listening intently, heard the faint echo of a long-drawn, whining cry. After that came silence, heavy and ominous. But Henry only laughed in noiseless mirth. All this he had expected. He knew that the larger

party to which the two warriors belonged would find the bodies, with
hasty pursuit to follow after the single cry. That was why he lingered.
He wanted them to pursue, to hang upon his trail in the vain hope that
they could catch him; he would play with them, he would enjoy the
game leading them on until they were exhausted, and then, laughing,
he would go on to the south at his utmost speed.

A new impulse drove him to another step in the daring play, and,
raising his head, he uttered his own war cry, a long piercing shout that
died in distant echoes; it was at once a defiance, and an intimation to
them where they might find him, and then, mirth in his eyes, he resumed his flight, although, for the present, he chose to keep an un-
changing distance between his pursuers and himself.

That party of warriors may have pursued many a man before and
may have caught most of them, but the greatest veteran of them all had
never hung on the trail of such another annoying fugitive. All day he
led them in swift flight toward the south, and at no time was he more
than a little beyond their reach; often they thought their hands were
about to close down upon him, that soon they would enjoy the sight of
his writhings under the fagot and the stake, but always he slipped away
at the fatal moment, and their savage hearts were filled with bitterness
that a lone fugitive should taunt them so. His footsteps were those of
the white man, but his wile and cunning were those of the red, and curiosity was added to the other motives that drew them on.

At the coming of the twilight one of their best warriors who pursued at some distance from the main band was slain by a rifle shot from
the bushes, then came that defiant war cry again, faint, but full of irony
and challenge, and then the trail grew cold before them. He whom they
pursued was going now with a speed that none of them could equal, and
the darkness itself, thick and heavy, soon covered all sign of his flight.

Henry Ware's expectations of joy had been fulfilled and more; it was the keenest delight that had yet come into his life. At all times he had been master of the situation, and as he drew them southward, he fulfilled his duty at the same time and enjoyed his sport. Everything had fallen out as he planned, and now, with the night at hand, he shook them off.

Through the day he had eaten dried venison from his pouch, as he ran, and he felt no need to stop for food. So, he did not cease the flight until after midnight when he lay down again in a thicket and slept soundly until daylight. He rose again, refreshed, and faster than ever sped on his swift way toward Wareville.

CHAPTER XIV
THE RETURN

WAREVILLE lay in its pleasant valley, rejoicing in the young spring, so kind with its warm rains that the men of the village foresaw a great season for crops. The little river flowed in a silver current, smoke rose from many chimneys, and now and then the red homemade linsey dress of a girl gleamed in the sunlight like the feathers of the scarlet tanager. To the left were the fields cleared for Indian corn, and to the right were the gardens. Beyond both were the hills and the unbroken forest.

Now and then a man, carrying on his shoulder the inevitable Kentucky rifle, long and slender-barreled, passed through the palisade, but the cardinal note of the scene was peace and cheerfulness. The town was prospering, its future no longer belonged to chance; there would be plenty, of the kind that they liked.

In the Ware house was a silent sadness, silent because these were stern people, living in a stern time, and it was the custom to hide one's griefs. The oldest son was gone; whether he had perished nobody knew, nor, if he had perished, how.

John Ware was not an emotional man, feelings rarely showed on his face, and his wife alone knew how hard the blow had been to him--she knew because she had suffered from the same stroke. But the children, the younger brother Charles and the sister Mary could not always remember, and with them the impression of the one who was gone would grow dimmer in time. The border too always expected a certain percentage of loss in human life, it was one of the facts with which the people must reckon, and thus the name of Henry Ware was rarely spoken.

To-day was without a cloud. New emigrants had come across the mountains, adding welcome strength to the colony, and extending the limits of the village. But danger had passed them by, they had heard once or twice more of the great war in the far-away East, but it was so distant and vague that most of them forgot it; the Indians across the Ohio had never come this way, and so far Henry Ware was the only toll that they had paid to the wilderness. There was cause for happiness, as human happiness goes.

A slim girl bearing in her hand a wooden pail came through the gate of the palisade. She was bare-headed, but her wonderful dark-brown hair coiled in a shining mass was touched here and there with golden gleams where the sunshine fell upon it. Her face, browned somewhat, was yet very white on the forehead, and the cheeks had the crimson flush of health. She wore a dress of homemade linsey dyed red, and its close fit suggested the curves of her supple, splendid young figure. She walked with strong elastic step toward the spring that gushed from a hillside, and which after a short course fell into the little river.

It was Lucy Upton, grown much taller now, as youth develops rapidly on the border, a creature nourished into physical perfection first by the good blood that was in her, then developed in the open air, and by work, neither too little nor too much.

She reached the spring, and setting the pail by its side looked down at the cool, gushing stream. It invited her and she ran her white rounded arm through it, making curves and oblongs that were gone before they were finished. She was in a thoughtful mood. Once or twice she looked at the forest, and each time that she looked she shivered because the shadow of the wilderness was then very heavy upon her.

Silas Pennypacker, the schoolmaster, came to the spring while she was there, and they spoke together, because they were great friends, these two. He was unchanged, the same strong gray man, with the ruddy face. He was not unhappy here despite the seeming incongruity of his presence. The wilderness appealed to him too in a way, he was the intellectual leader of the colony and almost everything that his nature called for met with a response.

"The spring is here, Lucy," he said, "and it has been an easy winter. We should be thankful that we have fared so well."

"I think that most of us are," she replied. "We'll soon be a big town."

She glanced at the spreading settlement, and this launched Mr. Pennypacker upon a favorite theme of his. He liked to predict how the colony would grow, sowing new seed, and already he saw great cities to be. He found a ready listener in Lucy. This too appealed to her imagination at times, and if at other times interest was lacking, she was too fond of the old man to let him know it. Presently when she had finished she filled the pail and stood up, straight and strong.

"I will carry it for you," said the schoolmaster.

She laughed.

"Why should I let you?" she asked. "I am more able than you."

Most men would have taken it ill to have heard such words from a girl, but she was one among many, above the usual height for her years; she created at once the impression of great strength, both physical and mental; the heavy pail of water hung in her hand, as if it were a trifle that she did not notice. The master smiled and looked at her with eyes of fatherly admiration.

"I must admit that you tell the truth," he said. "This West of ours seems to suit you."

"It is my country now," she said, "and I do not care for any other."

"Since you will not let me carry the water you will at least let me walk with you?" he said.

She did not reply, and he was startled by the sudden change that came over her.

First a look of wonder showed on her face, then she turned white, every particle of color leaving her cheeks. The master could not tell what her expression meant, and he followed her eyes which were turned toward the wilderness.

From the forest came a figure very strange to Silas Pennypacker, a figure of barbaric splendor. It was a youth of great height and powerful frame, his face so brown that it might belong to either the white or the red race, but with fine clean features like those of a Greek god. He was clad in deerskins, ornamented with little colored beads and fringes of brilliant dyes. He carried a slender-barreled rifle over his shoulder, and he came forward with swift, soundless steps.

The master recoiled in alarm at the strange and ominous figure, but as the red flooded back into the girl's cheeks she put her hand upon his arm.

"It is he! I knew that he was not dead!" she said in an intense tremulous whisper. The words were indefinite, but the master knew whom she meant, and there was a surge of joy in his heart, to be followed the next moment by doubt and astonishment. It was Henry Ware who had come back, but not the same Henry Ware.

Henry was beside them in a moment and he seized their hands, first the hands of one and then of the other, calling them by name.

The master recovering from his momentary diffidence threw his arms around his former pupil, welcomed him with many words, and wanted to know where he had been so long.

"I shall tell you, but not now," replied Henry, "because there is no time to spare; you are threatened by a great danger. The Shawnees are coming with a thousand warriors and I have hastened ahead to warn you."

He hurried them inside the palisade, his manner tense, masterful and convincing, and there he met his mother, whose joy, deep and grateful, was expressed in few words after the stern Puritan code. The father and the brother and sister came next, but the younger people like Lucy felt a little fear of him, and his old comrade Paul Cotter scarcely knew him.

He told in a few words of his escape from a far Northwestern tribe, of the coming of the Shawnees, and of the need to take every precaution for defense.

"There is no time to spare," he said. "All must be called in at once."

A man with powerful lungs blew long on a cow's horn, those who were at work in the fields and the forest hastened in, the gates were barred, the best marksmen were sent to watch in the upper story of the blockhouses and at the palisade, and the women began to mold bullets.

Henry Ware was the pervading spirit through all the preparations. He knew everything and thought of everything, he told them the mode of Indian attack and how they could best meet it, he compelled them to strengthen the weak spots in the palisade, and he encouraged all those who were faint of heart and apprehensive.

Lucy's slight fear of him remained, but with it now came admiration. She saw that his was a soul fit to lead and command, the work that he was about to do he loved, his eyes were alight with the fire of battle; a certain joy was shining there, and all, feeling the strength of his spirit, obeyed him without asking why.

Only Braxton Wyatt uttered doubts with words and sneered with looks. He too had become a hunter of skill, and hence what he said might have some merit.

"It seems strange that Henry Ware should come so suddenly when he might have come before," he remarked with apparent carelessness to Lucy Upton.

She looked at him with sharp interest. The same thought had entered her mind, but she did not like to hear Braxton Wyatt utter it.

"At all events he is about to save us from a great danger," she said.

Wyatt laughed and his thin long features contracted in an ugly manner.

"It is a tale to impress us and perhaps to cover up something else," he replied. "There is not an Indian within two hundred miles of us. I know, I have been through the woods and there is no sign."

She turned away, liking his words little and his manner less. She stopped presently by a corner of one of the houses on a slight elevation whence she could see a long distance beyond the palisade. So far as seeming went Braxton Wyatt was certainly right. The spring day was full of golden sunshine, the fresh new green of the forest was unsullied, and it was hard to conjure up even the shadow of danger.

Wyatt might have ground for his suspicion, but why should Henry Ware sound a false alarm? The words "perhaps to cover up something else" returned to her mind, but she dismissed them angrily.

She went to the Ware house and rejoiced with Mrs. Ware, to whom a son had come back from the dead, and in whose joy there was no flaw. According to her mother's heart a wonder had been performed, and it had been done for her special benefit.

The village was in full posture of defense, all were inside the walls and every man had gone to his post. They now awaited the attack, and yet there was some distrust of Henry Ware. Braxton Wyatt, a clever youth, had insidiously sowed the seeds of suspicion, and already there was a crop of unbelief. By indirection he had called attention to the strange appearance of the returned wanderer, the Indianlike air that he had acquired, his new ways unlike their own, and his indifference to many things that he had formerly liked. He noticed the change in Henry Ware's nature and he brought it also to the notice of others.

It seemed as the brilliant day passed peacefully that Wyatt was right and Henry, for some hidden purpose of his own, perhaps to hide the secret of his long absence, had brought to them this sounding alarm. There was the sun beyond the zenith in the heavens, the shadows of afternoon were falling, and the yellow light over the forest softened into gray, but no sign of an enemy appeared.

If Henry Ware saw the discontent he did not show his knowledge; the light of the expected conflict was still in his eyes and his thoughts were chiefly of the great event to come; yet in an interval of waiting he went back to the house and told his mother of much that had befallen him during his long absence; he sought to persuade himself now that he could not have escaped earlier, and perhaps without intending it he created in her mind the impression that he sought to engrave upon his own; so she was fully satisfied, thankful for the great mercy of his return that had been given to her.

"Now mother!" he said at last, "I am going outside."

"Outside!" she cried aghast, "but you are safe here! Why not stay?"

He smiled and shook his head.

"I shall be safe out there, too," he said, "and it is best for us all that I go. Oh, I know the wilderness, mother, as you know the rooms of this house!"

He kissed her quickly and turned away. John Ware, who stood by, said nothing. He felt a certain fear of his son and did not yet know how to command him.

As Henry passed from the house into the little square Lucy Upton overtook him.

"Where are you going?" she asked.

"I think I can be of more help out there than in here," he replied pointing toward the forest.

"It would be better for you to stay," she said.

"I shall be in no danger."

"It is not that; do you know what some of them here are saying of you--that you are estranged from us, that there is some purpose in this, that no attack is coming! Your going now will confirm them in the belief."

His dark eyes flashed with a fierceness that startled her, and his whole frame seemed to draw up as if he were about to spring. But the emotion passed in a moment, and his face was a brown mask, saying nothing. He seemed indifferent to the public opinion of his little world.

"I am needed out there," he said, pointing again toward the dark line of the forest, "and I shall go. Whether I tell the truth or not will soon be known; they will have to wait only a little. But you believe me now, don't you?"

She looked deep into his calm eyes, and she read there only truth. But she knew even before she looked that Henry Ware was not one who would ever be guilty of falsehood or treachery.

"Oh yes I know it," she replied, "but I wish others to know it as well."

"They will," he said, and then taking her hand in his for one brief moment he was gone. His disappearance was so sudden and soundless that he seemed to her to melt away from her sight like a mist before the wind. She did not even know how he had passed through the palisade, but he was certainly outside and away. There was something weird about it and she felt a little fear, as if an event almost supernatural had occurred.

The sudden departure of Henry Ware to the forest started the slanderous tongues to wagging again, and they said it was a trap of some kind, though no one could tell how. A sly report was started that he had become that worst of all creatures in his time, a renegade, a white man who allied himself with the red to make war upon his own people. It came to the ears of Paul Cotter, and the heart of the loyal youth grew hot within him. Paul was not fond of war and strife, but he had an abounding courage, and he and Henry Ware had been through danger together.

"He is changed, I will admit," he said, "but if he says we are going to be attacked, we shall be. I wish that all of us were as true as he."

He touched his gun lock in a threatening manner, and Braxton Wyatt and the others who stood by said no more in his presence. Yet the course of the day was against Henry's assertion. The afternoon waned, the sun, a ball of copper, swung down into the west, long shadows fell and nothing happened.

The people moved and talked impatiently inside their wooden walls. They spoke of going about their regular pursuits, there was work that could be done on the outside in the twilight, and enough time had been lost already through a false alarm. But some of the older men, with cautious blood, advised them to wait and their counsel was taken. Night came, thick and black, and to the more timid full of omens and presages.

The forest sank away in the darkness, nothing was visible fifty yards from the palisade and in the log houses few lights burned. The little colony, but a pin point of light, was alone in the vast and circling wilderness. One of the greatest tests of courage to which the human race has ever been subjected was at hand. In all directions the forest curved away, hundreds of miles. It would be a journey of days to find any other of their own kind, they were hemmed in everywhere by silence and loneliness, whatever happened they must depend upon themselves, because there was none to bring help. They might perish, one and all, and the rest of the world not hear of it until long afterwards.

A moaning wind came up and sighed over the log houses, the younger children--and few were too young not to guess what was expected--fell asleep at last, but the older, those who had reached their thinking years could not find such solace. In this black darkness their fears became real; there was no false alarm, the forest around them hid their enemy, but only for the time.

There was little noise in the station. By the low fires in the houses the women steadily molded bullets, and seldom spoke to each other, as they poured the melted lead into the molds. By the walls the men too, rifle in hand, were silent, as they sought with intent eyes to mark what was passing in the forest.

Lucy Upton was molding bullets in her father's house and they were melting the lead at a bed of coals in the wide fireplace. None was steadier of hand or more expert than she. Her face was flushed as she bent over the fire and her sleeves were rolled back, showing her strong white arms. Her lips were compressed, but as the bullets shining like silver dropped from the mold they would part now and then in a slight smile. She too had in her the spirit of warlike ancestors and it was aroused now. Girl, though she was, she felt in her own veins a little of the thrill of coming conflict.

But her thoughts were not wholly of attack and defense; they followed as well him who had come back so suddenly and who was now gone again into the wilderness from which he had emerged. His appearance and manner had impressed her deeply. She wished to hear more from him of the strange wild life that he had led; she too felt, although in a more modified form, the spell of the primeval.

Her task finished she went to the door, and then drawn by curiosity she continued until her walk brought her near the palisade where she watched the men on guard, their dusky figures touched by the wan light that came from the slender crescent of a moon, and seeming altogether weird and unreal. Paul Cotter in one of his errands found her there.

"You had better go back," he said. "We may be attacked at any time, and a bullet or arrow could reach you here."

"So you believe with me that an attack will be made as he said!"

"Of course I do," replied Paul with emphasis. "Don't I know Henry Ware? Weren't he and I lost together? Wasn't he the truest of comrades?"

Several men, talking in low tones, approached them. Braxton Wyatt was with them and Lucy saw at once that it was a group of malcontents.

"It is nothing," said Seth Lowndes, a loud, arrogant man, the boaster of the colony. "There are no Indians in these parts and I'm going out there to prove it."

He stood in the center of a ray of moonlight, as he spoke, and it lighted up his red sneering face. Lucy and Paul could see him plainly and each felt a little shiver of aversion. But neither said anything and, in truth, standing in the dark by themselves they were not noticed by the others.

"I'm going outside," repeated Lowndes in a yet more noisy tone, "and if I run across anything more than a deer I'll be mighty badly fooled!"

One or two uttered words of protest, but it seemed to Lucy that Braxton Wyatt incited him to go on, joining him in words of contempt for the alleged danger.

Lowndes reached the palisade and climbed upon it by means of the cross pieces binding it together, and then he stood upon the topmost bar, where his head and all his body, above the knees, rose clear of the bulwark. He was outlined there sharply, a stout, puffy man, his face redder than ever from the effect of climbing, and his eyes gleaming triumphantly as, from his high perch, he looked toward the forest.

"I tell you there is not--" But the words were cut short, the gleam died from his eyes, the red fled from his face, and he whitened suddenly with terror. From the forest came a sharp report, echoing in the still night, and the puffy man, throwing up his arms, fell from the palisade back into the inclosure, dead before he touched the ground.

A fierce yell, the long ominous note of the war whoop burst from the forest, and its sound, so full of menace and fury, was more terrible than that of the rifle. Then came other shots, a rapid pattering volley, and bullets struck with a low sighing sound against the upper walls of the blockhouse. The long quavering cry, the Indian yell rose and died again and in the black forest, still for aught else, it was weird and unearthly.

Lucy stood like stone when the lifeless body of the boaster fell almost at her feet, and all the color was gone from her face. The terrible cry of the savages without was ringing in her ears, and it seemed to her, for a few moments, that she could not move. But Paul grasped her by the arm and drew her back.

"Go into your house!" he cried. "A bullet might reach you here!"

Obedient to his duty he hastened to the palisade to bear a valiant hand in the defense, and she, retreating a little, remained in the shadow of the houses that she might see how events would go. After the first shock of horror and surprise she was not greatly afraid, and she was conscious too of a certain feeling of relief. Henry Ware had told the truth, he knew of what he spoke when he brought his warning, and he had greatly served his own.

CHAPTER XV
THE SIEGE

I T was not Lucy Upton alone who felt relief when the attack upon the stockade came, hideous and terrifying though it might be; the suspense so destructive of nerves and so hard to endure was at an end, and the men rushed gladly to meet the attack, while the women with almost equal joy reloaded empty rifles with the precious powder made from the cave dust and passed them to the brave defenders. The children, too small to take a part, cowered in the houses and listened to the sounds of battle, the lashing of the rifle fire, the fierce cry of the savages in the forest, and the answering defiance of the white men. Amid such scenes a great state was founded and who can wonder that its defenders learned to prize bravery first of all things?

The attack was in accordance with the savage nature, a dash, irregular volleys, shots from ambush, an endeavor to pick off the settlers, whenever a head was shown, but no direct attempt to storm the palisade, for which the Indian is unfitted. A bullet would not reach from the forest, but from little hillocks and slight ridges in the open where a brown breast was pressed close to the earth came the flash of rifles, some hidden by the dusk, but the flame showing in little points of fire that quickly went out. The light of the moon failed somewhat, and the savages in ambush were able to come nearer, but now and then a sharpshooter behind the wall, firing at the flash of the concealed rifle, would hear an answering death cry.

Lucy Upton behind the barricade with other girls and women was reloading rifles and passing them to her father and Paul Cotter who stood in a little wooden embrasure like a sally port. For a time the fire of battle burned as fiercely in her veins as in those of any man, but after a while she began to wonder what had become of Henry Ware, and presently from some who passed she heard comments upon him again; they found fault with his absence; he should have been there to take a part in the defense, and while she admitted that their criticisms bore the color of truth, she yet believed him to be away for some good purpose.

For two hours the wild battle in the dark went on, to the chorus of shouts from white man and red, the savages often coming close to the walls, and seeking to find a shelter under them in the dark, but always driven back. Then it ceased so suddenly that the intense silence was more pregnant with terror than all the noise that had gone before. Paul Cotter, looking over the palisade, could see nothing. The forest rose up like a solid dark wall, and in the opening not a blade of grass stirred; the battle, the savage army, all seemed to have gone like smoke melting into the air, and Paul was appalled, feeling that a magic hand had abruptly swept everything out of existence.

"What do you see?" asked Lucy, upon whose ears the silence too was heavy and painful.

"Nothing but darkness, and what it hides I cannot guess."

A report ran through the village that the savage army, beaten, had gone, and the women, and the men with little experience, gave it currency, but the veterans rebuked such premature rejoicing; it was their part, they said, to watch with more vigilance than ever, and in nowise to relax their readiness.

Then the long hours began and those who could, slept. Braxton Wyatt and his friends again impeached the credit of Henry Ware, insinuating with sly smiles that he must be a renegade, as he had taken no part in the defense and must now be with his savage friends. To the slur Paul Cotter fiercely replied that he had warned them of the attack; without him the station would have been taken by surprise, and that surely proved him to be no traitor.

The hours between midnight and day not only grew in length, but seemed to increase in number as well, doubling and tripling, as if they would never end for the watchers in the station. The men behind the wooden walls and some of the women, too, intently searched the forest, seeking to discover movements there, but nothing appeared upon its solid black screen. Nor did any sound come from it, save the occasional gentle moan of the wind; there was no crackling of branches, no noise of footsteps, no rattle of arms, but always the heavy silence which seemed so deadly, and which, by its monotony, was so painful to their ears.

Lucy Upton went into her father's house, ate a little and then spreading over herself a buffalo robe tried to sleep. Slumber was long in coming, for the disturbed nerves refused to settle into peace, and the excited brain brought back to her eyes distorted and overcolored visions of the night's events. But youth and weariness had their way and she slept at last, to find when she awakened that the dawn was coming in at the window, and the east was ablaze with the splendid red and yellow light of the sun.

"Are they still there?" was her first question when she went forth from her father's house, and the reply was uncertain; they might or might not be there; the leaders had not allowed anyone to go out to see, but the number who believed that the savages were gone was growing;

and also grew the number who believed that Henry Ware was gone with them.

Even in the brilliant daylight that sharpened and defined everything as with the etcher's point, they could see nothing save what had been before the savages came. Their eyes reached now into the forest, but as far as they ranged it was empty, there was no encampment, not a single warrior passed through the undergrowth. It seemed that the grumblers were right when they said the besieging army was gone.

Lucy Upton was walking toward the palisade where she saw Paul Cotter, when she heard a distant report and Paul's fur cap, pierced by a bullet, flew from his head to the earth. Paul himself stood in amaze, as if he did not know what had happened, and he did not move until Lucy shouted to him to drop to the ground. Then he crawled quickly away from the exposed spot, although two or three more bullets struck about him.

The station thrilled once more with excitement, but the new danger was of a kind that they did not know how to meet. It was evident that the firing came from a high point, one commanding a view inside the walls, and from marksmen located in such a manner the palisade offered no shelter. Bullets were pattering among the houses, and in the open spaces inclosed by the walls, two men were wounded already, and the threat had become formidable.

Ross and Shif'less Sol, the best of the woodsmen, soon decided that the shots came from a large tree at the edge of the forest northeast from the stockade, and they were sure that at least a half-dozen warriors were lying sheltered among its giant boughs, while they sent searching bullets into the inclosure. There had been some discussion about the tree at the time the settlement was built, but expert opinion held that the Indian weapons could not reach from so great a distance, and as the task of cutting so huge a trunk when time was needed, seemed too much they had left it, and now they saw their grievous and perhaps mortal error.

The side of the palisade facing the tree was untenable so long as the warriors held their position, and it was even dangerous to pass from one house to another. The terrors of the night, weighty because unknown, were gone, but the day had brought with it a more certain menace that all could see.

The leaders held a conference on the sheltered side of one of the houses, and their faces and their talk were full of gloom. The schoolmaster, Ross and Sol were there, and so were John Ware and Lucy's father. The schoolmaster, by nature and training a man of peace, was perhaps the most courageous of them all.

"It is evident that those savages have procured in some manner a number of our long-range Kentucky rifles," he said, "but they are no better than ours. Nor is it any farther from us to that tree than it is from that tree to us. Why can't our best marksmen pick them off?"

He looked with inquiry at Ross and Sol, who shook their heads and abated not a whit of their gloomy looks.

"They are too well sheltered there," replied Ross, "while we would not be if we should try to answer them. Our side would get killed while they wouldn't be hurt and we can't spare the men."

"But we must find a way out! We must get rid of them somehow!" exclaimed Mr. Ware.

"That's true," said Upton, and as he spoke they heard a bullet thud against the wall of the house. From the forest came a wild quavering yell of triumph, full of the most merciless menace. Mr. Ware and Mr. Upton shuddered. Each had a young daughter, and it was in the minds of each to slay her in the last resort if there should be no other way.

"If those fellows in the tree keep on driving us from the palisade," said Ross, setting his face in the grim manner of one who forces himself to tell the truth, "there's nothin' to prevent the main band from makin' an attack, and while the other fellows rain bullets on us they'll be inside the palisade."

They stared at each other in silent despair, and Ross going to the corner of the house, but keeping himself protected well, looked at the fatal tree. No one was firing, then, and he could see nothing among its branches. In the fresh green of its young foliage it looked like a huge cone set upon a giant stem, and Ross shook his fist at it in futile anger. Nor was a foe visible elsewhere. The entire savage army lay hidden in the forest and nothing fluttered or moved but the leaves and the grass.

The others, led by the same interest, followed Ross, and keeping to the safety of the walls, stole glances at the tree. As they looked they heard the faint report of a shot and a cry of death, and saw a brown body shoot down from the green cone of the tree to the ground, where it lay still.

"There is a marksman among us who can beat them at their own trick," cried the schoolmaster in exultation. "Who did it? Who fired that shot, Tom?"

Ross did not answer. First a look of wonder came upon his face, and then he began to study the forest, where all but nature was yet lifeless. The faint sound of a second shot came and what followed was a duplicate of the sequel to the first. Another brown body shot downward, and lay lifeless beside its fellow on the grass.

The master cried out once more in exultation, and wished to know why others within the palisade did not imitate the skillful sharpshooter. But Ross shook his head slowly and spoke these slow words:

"A great piece of luck has happened to us, Mr. Pennypacker, an' how it's happened I don't know, at least not yet. Them shots never come from any of our men. We've got a friend outside an' he's pickin' off them ambushed murderers one by one. The savages think we're doin' it, but they'll soon find out the difference."

There was a third shot and the tree ejected a third body.

"What wonderful shootin'!" exclaimed Ross in a tone of amazement. "Them shots come from a long distance, but all three of 'em plugged the mark to the center. Them savages was dead before they touched the ground. I never saw the like."

The others waited expectantly, as if he could give them an explanation, but if he had a thought in his mind he kept it to himself.

"There, they've found it out," he said, when a terrific yell full of anger came from the forest, "but they haven't got him, whoever he is. They'd shout in a different way if they had."

"Why do you say him?" asked Mr. Pennypacker. "Surely a single man has not been doing such daring and deadly work!"

"It's one man, because there are not two in all this wilderness who can shoot like that. I'd hate to be in the place of the savages left in that tree."

The wonder of the new and unknown ally soon spread through Wareville, and reached Lucy Upton as it reached others. A thought came to her and she was about to speak of it, but she stopped, fearing ridicule, and merely listened to the excited talk going on all about her.

An hour later a fourth Indian was shot from the tree, and less than fifteen minutes afterwards a fifth fell a victim to the terrible rifle. Then two, the only survivors, dropped from the boughs and ran for the forest. Ross, Sol and Paul Cotter were watching together and saw the flight.

"One of them brown rascals will never reach the woods," said Ross with the intuition of the borderer.

The foremost savage fell just at the edge of the forest, shot through the heart, and the other, the sole survivor of the tree, escaped behind the sheltering trunks.

The cry of the angry savages swelled into a terrible chorus and bullets beat upon the stockade, but the attack was quickly repulsed, and again quiet and treacherous peace settled down upon this little spot, this pin point in the mighty wilderness, whose struggle must be carried on unaided, and, in truth, unknown to all the rest of the world.

When the savages were driven back they melted again into the forest, and the old silence and peace laid hold of everything, the brilliant sunshine gilding every house, and dyeing into deeper colors the glowing tints of the wilderness. The huge tree, so fatal to those who had sought to use it, stood up, a great green cone, its branches waving softly before the wind.

In the little fortress the wonder and excitement yet prevailed, but mingled with it was a devout gratitude for this help from an unknown quarter which had been so timely and so effective. The spirits of the garrison, from the boldest ranger down to the most timid woman, took a sudden upward heave and they felt that they should surely repel every attack by the savage army.

The remainder of the day passed in silence and with the foe invisible, but the guard at the palisade, now safe from ambushed marksmen, relaxed its vigilance not at all. These men knew that they dealt with an enemy whose uncertainty made him all the more terrible, and they would not leave the issue to shifting chance.

The day waned, the night came, heavy and dark again, and full, as it was bound to be, of threats and omens for the beleaguered people. Lucy Upton with Mary Ware slipped to the little wooden embrasure where Paul Cotter was on watch.

They found Paul in the sheltered nook, watching the forest and the open, through the holes pierced for rifles, and he did not seek to hide his pleasure at seeing them. Two other men were there, but they were middle-aged and married, the fathers of increasing families, and they were not offended when Paul received a major share of attention.

He told them that all was quiet, his own eyes were keen, but they failed to mark anything unusual, and he believed that the savages, profiting by their costly experience, would make no new attempt yet a while. Then he spoke of the mysterious help that had come to them, and the same thought was in his mind and Lucy's, though neither spoke of it. They stood there a while, talking in low tones and looking for excuses to linger, when one of the older men moved a little and held up a warning hand. He had just taken his eyes from a loophole, and he whispered that he thought he had seen something pass in the shadow of the wall.

All in the embrasure became silent at once, and Lucy, brave as she was, could hear her heart beating. There was a slight noise on the outside of the wall, so faint that only keen ears could hear it, and then as they looked up they saw a hideous, painted face raised above the palisade.

One of the older men threw his rifle to his shoulder, but, quick as a flash, Paul struck his hand away from the trigger. He knew who had come, when he looked into the eyes that looked down at him, though he felt fear, too--he could not deny it--as he met their gaze, so fierce, so wild, so full of the primitive man.

"Don't you see?" he said, "it is Henry! Henry Ware!"

Even then Lucy Upton, intimate friend though she had been, scarcely saw, but laughing a low soft laugh of intense satisfaction, Henry dropped lightly among them. Good excuse had these men for not knowing him as his transformation was complete! He stood before them not a white man, but an Indian warrior, a prince of savages. His hair was drawn up in the defiant scalp lock, his face bore the war paint in all its variations and violent contrast of colors, the dark-green hunting shirt and leggings with their beaded decorations were gone, and in their place a red Indian blanket was wrapped around him, drooping in its graceful folds like a Roman toga.

His figure, erect in the moonlight, nearly a head above the others, had a certain savage majesty, and they gazed upon him in silence. He seemed to know what they felt and his eyes gleamed with pride out of his darkly painted face. He laughed again a low laugh, not like that of the white man, but the almost inaudible chuckle of the Indian.

"It had to be," he said, glancing down at his garb though not with shame. "To do what I wished to do, it was necessary to pass as an Indian, at least between times, and, as all the Shawnees do not know each other, this helped."

"It was you who shot the Indians in the tree; I knew it from the first," said the voice of the guide, Ross, over their shoulders. He had come so softly that they did not notice him before.

Henry did not reply, but laughed again the dry chuckle that made Lucy tremble she scarcely knew why, and ran his hand lovingly along the slender barrel of his rifle.

"At least you do not complain of it," he said presently.

"No, we do not," replied Ross, "an' I guess we won't. You saved us, that's sure. I've lived on the border all my life, but I never saw such shootin' before."

Then Henry gave some details of his work and Lucy Upton, watching him closely, saw how he had been engrossed by it. Paul Cotter too noticed, and feeling constraint, at least, demanded that Henry doff his savage disguise, put on white men's clothes and get something to eat.

He consented, though scarce seeing the necessity of it, but kept the Indian blanket close to hand, saying that he would soon need it again. But he was very gentle with his mother telling her that she need have no fear for him, that he knew all the wiles of the savage and more; they could never catch him and the outside was his place, as then he could be of far more service than if he were merely one of the garrison.

The news of Henry Ware's return was throughout the village in five minutes, and with it came the knowledge of his great deed. In the face of such a solid and valuable fact the vague charge that he was a renegade died. Even Braxton Wyatt did not dare to lift his voice to that effect again, but, with sly insinuation, he spoke of savages herding with savages, and of what might happen some day.

When night came Henry resuming his Indian garb and paint slipped out again, and so skillful was he that he seemed to melt away like a mist in the darkness.

The savage army beleaguering the colony now found that it was assailed by a mysterious enemy, one whom all their vigilance and skill could not catch. They lost warrior after warrior and many of them began to think Manitou hostile to them, but the leaders persisted with the siege. They wished to destroy utterly this white vanguard, and they would not return to their villages, far across the Ohio, until it was done.

They no longer made a direct attack upon the walls, but, forming a complete circle around, hung about at a convenient distance, waiting and hoping for thirst and famine to help them. The people believed themselves to have taken good precautions against these twin evils, but now a terrible misfortune befell them. No rain fell and the well inside the palisade ran dry. It was John Ware himself who first saw the coming of the danger and he tried to hide it, but it could not, from its very nature, be kept a secret long. The supply for each person was cut down one half and then one fourth, and that too would soon go, unless the welcome rains came; and the sky was without a cloud. Men who feared no physical danger saw those whom they loved growing pale and weak before their eyes, and they knew not what to do. It seemed that the place must fall without a blow from the enemy.

CHAPTER XVI
A GIRL'S WAY

LUCY left her father's house one of these dry mornings, and stood for a few moments in the grounds, inclosed by the palisade, gazing at the dark forest, outlined so sharply against the blue of the sky. She could see the green of the forest beyond the fort, and she knew that in the open spaces, where the sun reached them, tiny wild flowers of pink and purple, nestled low in the grass, were already in bloom. From the west a wind sweet and soft was blowing, and, as she inhaled it, she wanted to live, and she wanted all those about her to live. She wondered, if there was not some way in which she could help.

The stout, double log cabins, rude, but full of comfort, stood in rows, with well-trodden streets, between, then a fringe of grass around all, and beyond that rose the palisade of stout stakes, driven deep into the ground, and against each other. All was of the West and so was Lucy, a tall, lithe young girl, her face tanned a healthy and becoming brown by the sun, her clothing of home-woven red cloth, adorned at the wrists and around the bottom of the skirt with many tiny beads of red and yellow and blue and green, which, when she moved, flashed in the brilliant light, like the quivering colors of a prism. She had thrust in her hair a tiny plume of the scarlet tanager, and it lay there, like a flash of flame, against the dark brown of her soft curls.

Where she stood she could see the water of the spring near the edge of the forest sparkling in the sunlight, as if it wished to tantalize her, but as she looked a thought came to her, and she acted upon it at once. She went to the little square, where her father, John Ware, Ross and others were in conference.

"Father," she exclaimed, "I will show you how to get the water!"

Mr. Upton and the other men looked at her in so much astonishment that none of them replied, and Lucy used the opportunity.

"I know the way," she continued eagerly. "Open the gate, let the women take the buckets--I will lead--and we can go to the spring and fill them with water. Maybe the Indians won't fire on us!"

"Lucy, child!" exclaimed her father. "I cannot think of such a thing."

Then up spoke Tom Ross, wise in the ways of the wilderness.

"Mr. Upton," he said, "the girl is right. If the women are willing to go out it must be done. It looks like an awful thing, but--if they die we are here to avenge them and die with them, if they don't die we are all saved because we can hold this fort, if we have water; without it every soul here from the oldest man down to the littlest baby will be lost."

Mr. Upton covered his face with his hands.

"I do not like to think of it, Tom," he said.

The other men waited in silence.

Lucy looked appealingly at her father, but he turned his eyes away.

"See what the women say about it, Tom," he said at last.

The women thought well of it. There was not one border heroine, but many; disregarding danger they prepared eagerly for the task, and soon they were in line more than fifty, every one with a bucket or pail in each hand. Henry Ware, looking on, said nothing. The intended act appealed to the nature within him that was growing wilder every day.

A sentinel, peeping over the palisade, reported that all was quiet in the forest, though, as he knew, the warriors were none the less watchful.

"Open the gate," commanded Mr. Ware.

The heavy bars were quickly taken down, and the gate was swung wide. Then a slim, scarlet-clad figure took her place at the head of the line, and they passed out.

Lucy was borne on now by a great impulse, the desire to save the fort and all these people whom she knew and loved. It was she who had suggested the plan and she believed that it should be she who should lead the way, when it came to the doing of it.

She felt a tremor when she was outside the gate, but it came from excitement and not from fear--the exaltation of spirit would not permit her to be afraid. She glanced at the forest, but it was only a blur before her.

The slim, scarlet-clad figure led on. Lucy glanced over her shoulder, and she saw the women following her in a double file, grave and resolute. She did not look back again, but marched on straight toward the spring. She began to feel now what she was doing, that she was marching into the cannon's mouth, as truly as any soldier that ever led a forlorn hope against a battery. She knew that hundreds of keen eyes there in the forest before her were watching her every step, and that behind her fathers and brothers and husbands were waiting, with an anxiety that none of them had ever known before.

She expected every moment to hear the sharp whiplike crack of the rifle, but there was no sound. The fort and all about it seemed to be inclosed in a deathly stillness. She looked again at the forest, trying to see the ambushed figures, but again it was only a blur before her, seeming now and then to float in a kind of mist. Her pulses were beating fast, she could hear the thump, thump in her temples, but the slim scarlet figure never wavered and behind, the double file of women followed, grave and silent.

"They will not fire until we reach the spring," thought Lucy, and now she could hear the bubble of the cool, clear water, as it gushed from the hillside. But still nothing stirred in the forest, no rifle cracked, there was no sound of moving men.

She reached the spring, bent down, filled both buckets at the pool, and passing in a circle around it, turned her face toward the fort, and, after her, came the silent procession, each filling her buckets at the pool, passing around it and turning her face toward the fort as she had done.

Lucy now felt her greatest fear when she began the return journey and her back was toward the forest. There was in her something of the warrior; if the bullet was to find her she preferred to meet it, face to face. But she would not let her hands tremble, nor would she bend beneath the weight of the water. She held herself proudly erect and glanced at the wooden wall before her. It was lined with faces, brown, usually, but now with the pallor showing through the tan. She saw her father's among them and she smiled at him, because she was upheld by a great pride and exultation. It was she who had told them what to do, and it was she who led the way.

She reached the open gate again, but she did not hasten her foot-steps. She walked sedately in, and behind her she heard only the regular tread of the long double file of women. The forest was as silent as ever.

The last woman passed in, the gate was slammed shut, the heavy bars were dropped into place, and Mr. Upton throwing his arms about

Lucy exclaimed:

"Oh, my brave daughter!"

She sank against him trembling, her nerves weak after the long tension, but she felt a great pride nevertheless. She wished to show that a woman too could be physically brave in the face of the most terrible of all dangers, and she had triumphantly done so.

The bringing of the water, or rather the courage that inspired the act, heartened the garrison anew, and color came back to men's faces. The schoolmaster discussed the incident with Tom Ross, and wondered why the Indians who were not in the habit of sparing women had not fired.

"Sometimes a man or a crowd of men won't do a thing that they would do at any other time," said Ross, "maybe they thought they could get us all in a bunch by waitin' an' maybe way down at the bottom of their savage souls, was a spark of generosity that lighted up for just this once. We'll never know."

Henry Ware went out that night, and returning before dawn with the same facility that marked all his movements in the wilderness, reported that the savage army was troubled. All such forces are loose and irregular, with little cohesive power, and they will not bear disappointment and waiting. Moreover the warriors having lost many men, with nothing in repayment were grumbling and saying that the face of Manitou was set against them. They were confirmed too in this belief by the presence of the mysterious foe who had slain the warriors in the tree, and who had since given other unmistakable signs of his presence.

"They will have more discouragement soon," he said, "because it is going to rain to-day."

He had read the signs aright, as the sun came up amid the mists and vapors, and the gentle wind was damp to the face; then dark clouds spread across the western heavens, like a vast carpet unrolled by a giant hand, and the wilderness began to moan. Low thunder muttered on the horizon, and the somber sky was cut by vivid strokes of lightning.

Nature took on an ominous and threatening hue but within the village there was only joy; the coming storm would remove their greatest danger, the well would fill up again, and behind the wooden walls they could defy the savage foe.

The sky was cut across by a flash of lightning so bright that it dazzled them, the thunder burst with a terrible crash directly overhead, and then the rain came in a perfect wall of water. It poured for hours out of a sky that was made of unbroken clouds, deluging the earth, swelling the river to a roaring flood, and rising higher in the well than ever before. The forest about them was almost hidden by the torrents of rain and they did not forget to be thankful.

Toward afternoon the fall abated somewhat in violence, but became a steady downpour out of sodden skies, and the air turned raw and chill. Those who were not sheltered shivered, as if it were winter. The night came on as dark as a well, and Henry Ware went out again. When he came back he said tersely to his father:

"They are gone."

"Gone?" exclaimed Mr. Ware scarcely able to believe in the reality of such good news.

"Yes; the storm broke their backs. Even Indians can't stand an all-day wetting especially when they are already tired. They think they can never have any luck here, and they are going toward the Ohio at this minute. The storm has saved us now just as it saved our band in the flight from the salt works."

They had such faith in his forest skill that no one doubted his word and the village burst into joy. Women, for they were the worst sufferers gave thanks, both silently and aloud. Henry took Ross, Sol and others to the valley in the forest, where the savages had kept their war camp. Here they had soaked in the mire during the storm, and all about were signs of their hasty flight, the ground being littered with bones of deer, elk and buffalo.

"They won't come again soon," said Henry, "because they believe that the Manitou will not give them any luck here, but it is well to be always on the watch."

After the first outburst of gratitude the people talked little of the attack and repulse; they felt too deeply, they realized too much the greatness of the danger they had escaped to put it into idle words. But nearly all attributed their final rescue to Henry Ware though some saw the hand of God in the storm which had intervened a second time for the protection of the whites. Braxton Wyatt and his friends dared say nothing now, at least openly against Henry, although those who loved him most were bound to confess that there was something alien about him, something in which he differed from the rest of them.

But Henry thought little of the opinion, good or bad in which he was held, because his heart was turning again to the wilderness, and he and Ross went forth again to scout on the rear of the Indian force.

CHAPTER XVII
THE BATTLE IN THE FOREST

HENRY and Ross after their second scouting expedition reported that the great war band of the Shawnees was retreating slowly, in fact would linger by the way, and might destroy one or two smaller stations recently founded farther north. Instantly a new impulse flamed up among the pioneers of Wareville. The feeling of union was strong among all these early settlements, and they believed it their duty to protect their weaker brethren. They would send hastily to Marlowe the nearest and largest settlement for help, follow on the trail of the warriors and destroy them. Such a blow, as they might inflict, would spread terror among all the northwestern tribes and save Kentucky from many another raid.

Ross who was present in the council when the eager cry was raised shook his head and looked more than doubtful.

"They outnumber us four or five to one," he said, "an' when we go out in the woods against 'em we give up our advantage, our wooden walls. They can ambush us out there, an' surround us."

Mr. Ware added his cautious words to those of Ross, in whom he had great confidence. He believed it better to let the savage army go. Discouraged by its defeat before the palisades of Wareville it would withdraw beyond the Ohio, and, under any circumstances, a pursuit with greatly inferior numbers, would be most dangerous.

These were grave words, but they fell on ears that did not wish to listen. They were an impulsive people and a generous chord in their natures was touched, the desire to defend those weaker than themselves. A good-hearted but hot-headed man named Clinton made a fiery speech. He said that now was the time to strike a crushing blow at the Indian power, and he thought all brave men would take advantage of it.

That expression "brave men" settled the question; no one could afford to be considered aught else, and a little army poured forth from Wareville, Mr. Ware nominally in command, and Henry, Paul, Ross, Sol, and all the others there. Henry saw his mother and sister weeping at the palisade, and Lucy Upton standing beside them. His mother's face was the last that he saw when he plunged into the forest. Then he was again the hunter, the trailer and the slayer of men.

While they considered whether or not to pursue, Henry Ware had said nothing; but all the primitive impulses of man handed down from lost ages of ceaseless battle were alive within him; he wished them to go, he would show the way, the savage army would make a trail through the forest as plain to him as a turnpike to the modern dweller in a civilized land, and his heart throbbed with fierce exultation, when the decision to follow was at last given. In the forest now he was again at home, more so than he had been inside the palisade. Around him were all the familiar sights and sounds, the little noises of the wilderness that only the trained ear hears, the fall of a leaf, or the wind in the grass, and the odor of a wild flower or a bruised bough.

Brain and mind alike expanded. Instinctively he took the lead, not from ambition, but because it was natural; he read all the signs and he led on with a certainty to which neither Ross nor Shif'less Sol pretended to aspire. The two guides and hunters were near each other, and a look passed between them.

"I knew it," said Ross; "I knew from the first that he had in him the making of a great woodsman. You an' I, Sol, by the side of him, are just beginners."

Shif'less Sol nodded in assent.

"It's so," he said. "It suits me to follow where he leads, an' since we are goin' after them warriors, which I can't think a wise thing, I'm mighty glad he's with us."

Yet to one experienced in the ways of the wilderness the little army though it numbered less than a hundred men would have seemed formidable enough. Many youths were there, mere boys they would have been back in some safer land, but hardened here by exposure into the strength and courage of men. Nearly all were dressed in finely tanned deerskin, hunting shirt, leggings and moccasins, fringes on hunting shirt and leggings, and beads on moccasins. The sun glinted on the long slender, blue steel barrel of the Western rifle, carried in the hand of every man. At the belt swung knife and hatchet, and the eyes of all, now that the pursuit had begun, were intense, eager and fierce.

The sounds made by the little Western army, hid under the leafy boughs of the forest, gradually died away to almost nothing. No one spoke, save at rare intervals. The moccasins were soundless on the soft turf, and there was no rattle of arms, although arms were always ready. In front was Henry Ware, scanning the trail, telling with an infallible eye how old it was, where the enemy had lingered, and where he had hastened.

Mr. Pennypacker was there beside Paul Cotter. A man of peace he was, but when war came he never failed to take his part in it.

"Do you know him?" he asked of Paul, nodding toward Henry.

Paul understood.

"No," he replied, "I do not. He used to be my old partner, Henry Ware, but he's another now."

"Yes, he's changed," said the master, "but I am not surprised. I foresaw it long ago, if the circumstances came right."

On the second morning they were joined by the men from Marlowe who had been traveling up one side of a triangle, while the men of Wareville had been traveling up the other side, until they met at the point. Their members were now raised to a hundred and fifty, and, uttering one shout of joy, the united forces plunged forward on the trail with renewed zeal.

They were in dense forest, in a region scarcely known even to the hunters, full of little valleys and narrow deep streams. The Indian force had suddenly taken a sharp turn to the westward, and the knowledge of it filled the minds of Ross and Sol with misgivings.

"Maybe they know we're following 'em," said Ross; "an' for that reason they're turnin' into this rough country, which is just full of ambushes. If it wasn't for bein' called a coward by them hot-heads I'd say it was time for us to wheel right about on our own tracks, an' go home."

"You can't do nothin' with 'em," said Sol, "they wouldn't stand without hitchin', an' we ain't got any way to hitch 'em. There's goin' to be a scrimmage that people'll talk about for twenty years, an' the best you an' me can do, Tom, is to be sure to keep steady an' to aim true."

Ross nodded sadly and said no more. He looked down at the trail, which was growing fresher and fresher.

"They're slowin' up, Sol," he said at last, "I think they're waitin' for us. You spread out to the right and I'll go to the left to watch ag'in ambush. That boy, Henry Ware'll see everything in front."

In view of the freshening trail Mr. Ware ordered the little army to stop for a few moments and consider, and all, except the scouts on the flanks and in front, gathered in council. Before them and all around them lay the hills, steep and rocky but clothed from base to crest with dense forest and undergrowth. Farther on were other and higher hills, and in the distance the forests looked blue. Nothing about them stirred. They had sighted no game as they passed; the deer had already fled before the Indian army. The skies, bright and blue in the morning, were now overcast, a dull, somber, threatening gray.

"Men," said Mr. Ware, and there was a deep gravity in his tone, as became a general on the eve of conflict, "I think we shall be on the enemy soon or he will be on us. There were many among us who did not approve of this pursuit, but here we are. It is not necessary to say that we should bear ourselves bravely. If we fail and fall, our women and children are back there, and nothing will stand between them and savages who know no mercy. That is all you have to remember."

And then a little silence fell upon everyone. Suddenly the hot-heads realized what they had done. They had gone away from their wooden walls, deep into the unknown wilderness, to meet an enemy four or five times their numbers, and skilled in all the wiles and tricks of the forest. Every face was grave, but the knowledge of danger only strengthened them for the conflict. Hot blood became cool and cautious, and wary eyes searched the thickets everywhere. Rash and impetuous they may have been; but they were ready now to redeem themselves, with the valor, without which the border could not have been won.

Henry Ware had suddenly gone forward from the others, and the green forest swallowed him up, but every nerve and muscle of him was now ready and alert. He felt, rather than saw, that the enemy was at hand; and in his green buckskin he blended so completely with the forest that only the keenest sight could have picked him from the mass of foliage. His general's eye told him, too, that the place before them was made for a conflict which would favor the superior numbers. They had been coming up a gorge, and if beaten they would be crowded back in it upon each other, hindering the escape of one another, until they were cut to pieces.

The wild youth smiled; he knew the bravery of the men with him, and now their dire necessity and the thought of those left behind in the two villages would nerve them to fight. In his daring mind the battle was not yet lost.

A faint, indefinable odor met his nostrils, and he knew it to be the oil and paint of Indian braves. A deep red flushed through the brown of either cheek. Returning now to his own kind he was its more ardent partisan because of the revulsion, and the Indian scent offended him. He looked down and saw a bit of feather, dropped no doubt from some defiant scalp lock. He picked it up, held it to his nose a moment, and then, when the offensive odor assailed him again, he cast it away.

Another dozen steps forward, and he sank down in a clump of grass, blending perfectly with the green, and absolutely motionless. Thirty yards away two Shawnee warriors in all the savage glory of their war paint, naked save for breechcloths, were passing, examining the woods with careful eye. Yet they did not see Henry Ware, and, when they turned and went back, he followed noiselessly after them, his figure still hidden in the green wood.

The two Shawnees, walking lightly, went on up the valley which broadened out as they advanced, but which was still thickly clothed in forest and undergrowth. Skilled as they were in the forest, they probably never dreamed of the enemy who hung on their trail with a skill surpassing their own.

Henry followed them for a full two miles, and then he saw them join a group of Indians under the trees, whom he knew by their dress and bearing to be chiefs. They were tall, middle-aged, and they wore blankets of green or dark blue, probably bought at the British outposts. Behind them, almost hidden in the forest, Henry saw many other dark faces, eager, intense, waiting to be let loose on the foe, whom they regarded as already in the trap.

Henry waited, while the two scouts whom he had followed so well, delivered to the chief their message. He saw them beckon to the warriors behind them, speak a few words to them, and then he saw two savage forces slip off in the forest, one to the right and one to the left. On the instant he divined their purpose. They were to flank the little white army, while another division stood ready to attack in front. Then the ambush would be complete, and Henry saw the skill of the savage general whoever he might be.

The plan must be frustrated at once, and Henry Ware never hesitated. He must bring on the battle, before his own people were surrounded, and raising his rifle he fired with deadly aim at one of the chiefs who fell on the grass. Then the youth raised the wild and thrilling cry, which he had learned from the savages themselves, and sped back toward the white force.

The death cry of the Shawnee and the hostile war whoop rang together filling the forest and telling that the end of stealth and cunning, and the beginning of open battle were at hand.

Henry Ware was hidden in an instant by the green foliage from the sight of the Shawnees. Keen as were their eyes, trained as they were to noticing everything that moved in the forest, he had vanished from them like a ghost. But they knew that the enemy whom they had sought to draw into their snare had slipped his head out of it before the snare could be sprung. Their long piercing yell rose again and then died away in a frightful quaver. As the last terrible note sank the whole savage army rushed forward to destroy its foe.

As Henry Ware ran swiftly back to his friends he met both Ross and Sol, drawn by the shot and the shouts.

"It was you who fired?" asked Ross.

"Yes," replied Henry, "they meant to lay an ambush, but they will not have time for it now."

The three stood for a few moments under the boughs of a tree, three types of the daring men who guided and protected the van of the white movement into the wilderness. They were eager, intent, listening, bent slightly forward, their rifles lying in the hollow of their arms, ready for instant use.

After the second long cry the savage army gave voice no more. In all the dense thickets a deadly silence reigned, save for the trained ear. But to the acute hearing of the three under the tree came sounds that they knew; sounds as light as the patter of falling nuts, no more, perhaps, than the rustle of dead leaves driven against each other by a wind; but they knew.

"They are coming, and coming fast," said Henry. "We must join the main force now."

"They ought to be ready. That warning of yours was enough," said Ross.

Without another word they turned again, darted among the trees, and in a few moments reached the little white force. Mr. Ware, the nominal leader, taking alarm from the shot and cries, was already disposing his men in a long, scattering line behind hillocks, tree trunks, brushwood and every protection that the ground offered.

"Good!" exclaimed Ross, when he saw, "but we must make our line longer and thinner, we must never let them get around us, an' it's lucky now we've got steep hills on either side."

To be flanked in Indian battle by superior numbers was the most terrible thing that could happen to the pioneers, and Mr. Ware stretched out his line longer and longer, and thinner and thinner. Paul Cotter was full of excitement; he had been in deadly conflict once before, but his was a most sensitive temperament, terribly stirred by a foe whom he could yet neither see nor hear. Almost unconsciously, he placed himself by the side of Henry Ware, his old partner, to whom he now looked up as a son of battle and the very personification of forest skill.

"Are they really there, Henry?" he asked. "I see nothing and hear nothing."

"Yes," replied Henry, "they are in front of us scarcely a rifle shot away, five to our one."

Paul strained his eyes, but still he could see nothing, only the green waving forest, the patches of undergrowth, the rocks on the steep hills to right and left, and the placid blue sky overhead. It did not seem possible to him that they were about to enter into a struggle for life and for those dearer than life.

"Don't shoot wild, Paul," said Henry. "Don't pull the trigger, until you can look down the sights at a vital spot."

A few feet away from them, peering over a log and with his rifle ever thrust forward was Mr. Pennypacker, a schoolmaster, a graduate of a college, an educated and refined man, but bearing his part in the dark and terrible wilderness conflict that often left no wounded.

The stillness was now so deep that even the scouts could hear no sound in front. The savage army seemed to have melted away, into the air itself, and for full five minutes they lay, waiting, waiting, always waiting for something that they knew would come. Then rose the fierce quavering war cry poured from hundreds of throats, and the savage horde, springing out of the forests and thickets, rushed upon them.

Dark faces showed in the sunlight, brown figures, naked save for the breechcloth, horribly painted, muscles tense, flashed through the undergrowth. The wild yell that rose and fell without ceasing ran off in distant echoes among the hills. The riflemen of Kentucky, lying behind trees and hillocks, began to fire, not in volleys, not by order, but each man according to his judgment and his aim, and many a bullet flew true.

A sharp crackling sound, ominous and deadly, ran back and forth in the forest. Little spurts of fire burned for a moment against the green, and then went out, to give place to others. Jets of white smoke rose languidly and floated up among the trees, gathering by and by into a cloud, shot through with blue and yellow tints from sky and sun.

Henry Ware fired with deadly aim and reloaded with astonishing speed. Paul Cotter, by his side, was as steady as a rock, now that the suspense was over, and the battle upon them. The schoolmaster resting on one elbow was firing across his log.

But it is not Indian tactics to charge home, unless the enemy is frightened into flight by the war whoop and the first rush. The men of Wareville and Marlowe did not run, but stood fast, sending the bullets straight to the mark; and suddenly the Shawnees dropped down among the trees and undergrowth, their bodies hidden, and began to creep forward, firing like sharpshooters. It was now a test of skill, of eyesight, of hearing and of aim.

The forest on either side was filled with creeping forms, white or red, men with burning eyes seeking to slay each other, meeting in strife more terrible than that of foes who encounter each other in open conflict. There was something snakelike in their deadly creeping, only the moving grass to tell where they passed and sometimes where both white and red died, locked fast in the grip of one another. Everywhere it was a combat, confused, dreadful, man to man, and with no shouting now, only the crack of the rifle shot, the whiz of the tomahawk, the thud of the knife, and choked cries.

Like breeds like, and the white men came down to the level of the red. Knowing that they would receive no quarter they gave none. The white face expressed all the cunning, and all the deadly animosity of the red. Led by Henry Ware, Ross and Sol they practiced every device of forest warfare known to the Shawnees, and their line, which extended across the valley from hill to hill, spurted death from tree, bush, and rock.

To Paul Cotter it was all a nightmare, a foul dream, unreal. He obeyed his comrade's injunctions, he lay close to the earth, and he did not fire until he could draw a bead on a bare breast, but the work became mechanical with him. He was a high-strung lad of delicate sensibilities. There was in his temperament something of the poet and the artist, and nothing of the soldier who fights for the sake of mere fighting. The wilderness appealed to him, because of its glory, but the savage appealed to him not at all. In Henry's bosom there was respect for his red foes from whom he had learned so many useful lessons, and his heart beat faster with the thrill of strenuous conflict, but Paul was anxious for the end of it all. The sight of dead faces near him, not the lack of courage, more than once made him faint and dizzy.

Twice and thrice the Shawnees tried to scale the steep hillsides, and with their superior numbers swing around behind the enemy, but the lines of the borderers were always extended to meet them, and the bullets from the long-barreled rifles cut down everyone who tried to pass. It was always Henry Ware who was first to see a new movement, his eyes read every new motion in the grass, and foliage swaying in a new direction would always tell him what it meant. More than one of his comrades muttered to himself that he was worth a dozen men that day.

So fierce were the combatants, so eager were they for each other's blood that they did not notice that the sky, gray in the morning, then blue at the opening of battle, had now grown leaden and somber again. The leaves above them were motionless and then began to rustle dully in a raw wet wind out of the north. The sun was quite gone behind the clouds and drops of cold rain began to fall, falling on the upturned faces of the dead, red and white alike with just impartiality, the wind rose, whistled, and drove the cold drops before it like hail. But the combat still swayed back and forth in the leaden forest, and neither side took notice.

Mr. Ware remained near the center of the white line, and retained command, although he gave but few orders, every man fighting for himself and giving his own orders. But from time to time Ross and Sol or Henry brought him news of the conflict, perhaps how they had been driven back a little at one point, and perhaps how they gained a little at another point. He, too, a man of fifty and the head of a community, shared the emotions of those around him, and was filled with a furious zeal for the conflict.

The clouds thickened and darkened, and the cold drops were driven upon them by the wind, the rifle smoke, held down by the rain, made sodden banks of vapor among the trees; but through all the clouds of vapor burst flashes of fire, and the occasional triumphant shout or death cry of the white man or the savage.

Henry Ware looked up and he became conscious that not only clouds above were bringing the darkness, but that the day was waning. In the west a faint tint of red and yellow, barely discernible through the grayness, marked the sinking sun, and in the east the blackness of night was still advancing. Yet the conflict, as important to those engaged in it, as a great battle between civilized foes, a hundred thousand on a side, and far more fierce, yet hung on an even chance. The white men still stood where they had stood when the forest battle began, and the red men who had not been able to advance would not retreat.

Henry's heart sank a little at the signs that night was coming; it would be harder in the darkness to keep their forces in touch, and the superior numbers of the Shawnees would swarm all about them. It seemed to him that it would be best to withdraw a little to more open ground; but he waited a while, because he did not wish any of their movements to have the color of retreat. Moreover, the activity of the Shawnees rose just then to a higher pitch.

Figures were now invisible in the chill, wet dusk, fifty or sixty yards away, and the two lines came closer. The keenest eye could see nothing save flitting forms like phantoms, but the riflemen, trained to quickness, fired at them and more than once sent a fatal bullet. There were two lines of fire facing each other in the dark wood. The flashes showed red or yellow in the twilight or the falling rain, and the Indian yell of triumph whenever it arose, echoed, weird and terrible, through the dripping forest.

Henry stole to the side of his father.

"We must fall back," he said, "or in the darkness or the night, they will be sure to surround us and crush us."

Ross was an able second to this advice, and reluctantly Mr. Ware passed along the word to retreat. "Be sure to bring off all the wounded," was the order. "The dead, alas! must be abandoned to nameless indignities!"

The little white army left thirty dead in the dripping forest, and, as many more carried wounds, the most of which were curable, but it was as full of fight as ever. It merely drew back to protect itself against being flanked in the forest, and the faces of the borderers, sullen and determined, were still turned to the enemy.

Yet the line of fire was visibly retreating, and, when the Shawnee forces saw it, a triumphant yell was poured from hundreds of throats. They rushed forward, only to be driven back again by the hail of bullets, and Ross said to Mr. Ware: "I guess we burned their faces then."

"Look to the wounded! look to the wounded!" repeated Mr. Ware. "See that no man too weak is left to help himself."

They had gone half a mile when Henry glanced around for Paul. His eyes, trained to the darkness, ran over the dim forms about him. Many were limping and others already had arms in slings made from their hunting shirts, but Henry nowhere saw the figure of his old comrade. A fever of fear assailed him. One of two things had happened. Paul was either killed or too badly wounded to walk, and somehow in the darkness they had missed him. The schoolmaster's face blanched at the news. Paul had been his favorite pupil.

"My God!" he groaned, "to think of the poor lad in the hands of those devils!"

Henry Ware stood beside the master, when he uttered these words, wrenched by despair from the very bottom of his chest. Pain shot through his own heart, as if it had been touched by a knife. Paul, the well-beloved comrade of his youth, captured and subjected to the torture! His blood turned to ice in his veins. How could they ever have missed the boy? Paul now seemed to Henry at least ten years younger than himself. It was not merely the fault of a single man, it was the fault of them all. He stared back into the thickening darkness, where the flashes of flame burst now and then, and, in an instant, he had taken his resolve.

"I do not know where Paul is," he said, "but I shall find him."

"Henry! Henry! what are you going to do?" cried his father in alarm.

"I'm going back after him," replied his son.

"But you can do nothing! It is sure death! Have we just found you to lose you again?"

Henry touched his father's hand. It was an act of tenderness, coming from his stoical nature, and the next instant he was gone, amid the smoke and the vapors and the darkness, toward the Indian army.

Mr. Ware put his face in his hands and groaned, but the hand of Ross fell upon his shoulder.

"The boy will come back, Mr. Ware," said the guide, "an' will bring the other with him, too. God has given him a woods cunnin' that none of us can match."

Mr. Ware let his hands fall, and became the man again. The retreating force still fell back slowly, firing steadily by the flashes at the pursuing foe.

Henry Ware had not gone more than fifty yards before he was completely hidden from his friends. Then he turned to a savage, at least in appearance. He threw off the raccoon-skin cap and hunting shirt, drew up his hair in the scalp lock, tying it there with a piece of fringe from his discarded hunting shirt, and then turned off at an angle into the woods. Presently he beheld the dark figures of the Shawnees, springing from tree to tree or bent low in the undergrowth, but all following eagerly. When he saw them he too bent over and fired toward his own comrades, then he whirled again to the right, and sprang about as if he were seeking another target. To all appearances, he was, in the darkness and driving rain, a true Shawnee, and the manner and gesture of an Indian were second nature to him.

But he had little fear of being discovered at such a time. His sole thought was to find his comrade. All the old days of boyish companionship rushed upon him, with their memories. The tenderness in his nature was the stronger, because of its long repression. He would find him and if he were alive, he would save him; moreover he had what he thought was a clew. He had remembered seeing Paul crouched behind a log, firing at the enemy, and no one had seen him afterwards. He believed that the boy was lying there yet, slain, or, if fate were kinder, too badly wounded to move. The line of retreat had slanted somewhat from the spot, and the savages might well have passed, in the dark, without noticing the boy's fallen body.

His own sense of direction was perfect, and he edged swiftly away toward the fallen log, behind which Paul had lain. Many dark forms passed him, but none sought to stop him; the counterfeit was too good; all thought him one of themselves.

Presently Henry passed no more of the flitting warriors. The battle was moving on toward the south and was now behind him. He looked back and saw the flashes growing fainter and heard the scattering rifle shots, deadened somewhat by the distance. Around him was the beat of the rain on the leaves and the sodden earth, and he looked up at a sky, wholly hidden by black clouds. He would need all his forest lore, and all the primitive instincts, handed down from far-off ancestors. But never were they more keenly alive than on this night.

The boy did not veer from the way, but merely by the sense of direction took a straight path toward the fallen log that he remembered. The din of battle still rolled slowly off toward the south, and, for the moment, he forgot it. He came to the log, bent down and touched a cold face. It was Paul. Instinctively his hand moved toward the boy's head and when it touched the thick brown hair and nothing else, he uttered

a little shuddering sigh of relief. Dead or alive, the hideous Indian trophy had not been taken. Then he found the boy's wrist and his pulse,
which was still beating faintly. The deft hands moved on, and touched
the wound, made by a bullet that had passed entirely through his shoulder. Paul had fainted from loss of blood, and without the coming of help
would surely have been dead in another hour.

The boy lay on his side, and, in some convulsion as he lost consciousness, he had drawn his arm about his head. Henry turned him
over until the cold reviving rain fell full upon his face, and then, raising
himself again, he listened intently. The battle was still moving on to the
southward, but very slowly, and stray warriors might yet pass and see
them. The tie of friendship is strong, and as he had come to save Paul
and as he had found him too, he did not mean to be stopped now.

He stooped down and chafed the wounded youth's wrists and temples, while the rain with its vivifying touch still drove upon his face.
Paul stirred and his pulse grew stronger. He opened his eyes catching
one vague glimpse of the anxious face above him, but he was so feeble
that the lids closed down again. But Henry was cheered. Paul was not
only alive, he was growing stronger, and, bending down, he lifted him
in his powerful arms. Then he strode away in the darkness, intending
to pass in a curve around the hostile army. Despite Paul's weight he was
able also to keep his rifle ready, because none knew better than he that
all the chances favored his meeting with one warrior or more before
the curve was made. But he was instinct with strength both mental and
physical, he was the true type of the borderer, the men who faced with
sturdy heart the vast dangers of the wilderness, the known and the unknown. At that moment he was at his highest pitch of courage and skill,
alone in the darkness and storm, surrounded by the danger of death and
worse, yet ready to risk everything for the sake of the boy with whom

he had played.

He heard nothing but the patter of the distant firing, and all around him was the gloom, of a night, dark to intensity. The rain poured steadily out of a sky that did not contain a single star. Paul stirred occasionally on his shoulder, as he advanced, swiftly, picking his way through the forest and the undergrowth. A half mile forward and his ears caught a light footstep. In an instant he sank down with his burden, and as he did so he caught sight of an Indian warrior, not twenty feet away. The Shawnee saw him at the same time, and he, too, dropped down in the undergrowth.

Henry did not then feel the lust of blood. He would have been willing to pass on, and leave the Shawnee to himself; but he knew that the Shawnee would not leave him. He laid Paul upon his back, in order that the rain might beat upon his face, and then crouched beside him, absolutely motionless, but missing nothing that the keenest eye or ear might detect. It was a contest of patience, and the white youth brought to bear upon it both the red man's training and his own.

A half hour passed, and within that small area there was no sound but the beat of the rain on the leaves and the sticky earth. Perhaps the warrior thought he had been deceived; it was merely an illusion of the night that he thought he saw; or if he had seen anyone the man was now gone, creeping away through the undergrowth. He stirred among his own bushes, raised up a little to see, and gave his enemy a passing glimpse of his face. But it was enough; a rifle bullet struck him between the eyes and the wilderness fighter lay dead in the forest.

Henry bestowed not a thought on the slain warrior, but, lifting up Paul once more, continued on his wide curve, as if nothing had happened. No one interrupted him again, and after a while he was parallel with the line of fire. Then he passed around it and came to rocky ground, where he laid Paul down and chafed his hands and face. The wounded boy opened his eyes again, and, with returning strength, was now able to keep them open.

"Henry!" he said in a vague whisper.

"Yes, Paul, it is I," Henry replied quietly.

Paul lay still and struggled with memory. The rain was now ceasing, and a few shafts of moonlight, piercing through the clouds, threw silver rays on the dripping forest.

"The battle!" said Paul at last. "I was firing and something struck me. That was the last I remember."

He paused and his face suddenly brightened. He cast a look of gratitude at his comrade.

"You came for me?" he said.

"Yes," replied Henry, "I came for you, and I brought you here."

Paul closed his eyes, lay still, and then at a ghastly thought, opened his eyes again.

"Are only we two left?" he asked. "Are all the others killed? Is that why we are hiding here in the forest?"

"No," replied Henry, "we are holding them off, but we decided that it was wiser to retreat. We shall join our own people in the morning."

Paul said no more, and Henry sheltered him as best he could under the trees. The wet clothing he could not replace, and that would have to be endured. But he rubbed his body to keep him warm and to induce circulation. The night was now far advanced, and the distant firing became spasmodic and faint. After a while it ceased, and the weary combatants lay on their arms in the thickets.

The clouds began to float off to the eastward. By and by all went down under the horizon, and the sky sprang out, a solid dome of calm, untroubled blue, in which the stars in myriads twinkled and shone. A moon of unusual splendor bathed the wet forest in a silver dew.

Henry sat in the moonlight, watching beside Paul, who dozed or fell into a stupor. The moonlight passed, the darkest hours came and then up shot the dawn, bathing a green world in the mingled glory of red and gold. Henry raised Paul again, and started with him toward the thickets, where he knew the little white army lay.

*   *   *   *   *

John Ware had borne himself that night like a man, else he would not have been in the place that he held. But his heart had followed his son, when he turned back toward the savage army, and, despite the reassuring words of Ross, he already mourned him as one dead. Yet he was faithful to his greater duty, remembering the little force that he led and the women and children back there, of whom they were the chief and almost the sole defenders. But if he reached Wareville again how could he tell the tale of his loss? There was one to whom no excuse would seem good. Often Mr. Pennypacker was by his side, and when the darkness began to thin away before the moonlight these two men exchanged sad glances. Each understood what was in the heart of the other, but neither spoke.

The hours of night and combat dragged heavily. When the waning fire of the savages ceased they let their own cease also, and then sought ground upon which they might resist any new attack, made in the day-light. They found it at last in a rocky region that doubled the powers of the defense. Ross was openly exultant.

"We scorched 'em good yesterday an' to-night," he said, "an' if they come again in the day we'll just burn their faces away."

Most of the men, worn to the bone, sank down to sleep on the wet ground in their wet clothes, while the others watched, and the few hours, left before the morning, passed peacefully away.

At the first sunlight the men were awakened, and all ate cold food which they carried in their knapsacks. Mr. Ware and the schoolmaster sat apart. Mr. Ware looked steadily at the ground and the schoolmaster, whose heart was wrenched both with his own grief and his friend's, knew not what to say. Neither did Ross nor Sol disturb them for the moment, but busied themselves with preparations for the new defense.

Mr. Pennypacker was gazing toward the southwest and suddenly on the crest of a low ridge a black and formless object appeared between him and the sun. At first he thought it was a mote in his eye, and he rubbed the pupils but the mote grew larger, and then he looked with a new and stronger interest. It was a man; no, two men, one carrying the other, and the motion of the man who bore the other seemed familiar. The master's heart sprang up in his throat, and the blood swelled in a new tide in his veins. His hand fell heavily, but with joy, on the shoulder of Mr. Ware.

"Look up! Look up!" he cried, "and see who is coming!"

Mr. Ware looked up and saw his son, with the wounded Paul Cotter on his shoulder, walking into camp. Then--the borderers were a pious people--he fell upon his knees and gave thanks. Two hours later the Shawnees in full force made a last and desperate attack upon the little white army. They ventured into the open, as venture they must to reach the defenders, and they were met by the terrible fire that never missed. At no time could they pass the deadly hail of bullets, and at last, leaving the ground strewed with their dead, they fell back into the forest, and then, breaking into a panic, did not cease fleeing until they had crossed the Ohio. Throughout the morning Henry Ware was one of the deadliest sharpshooters of them all, while Paul Cotter lay safely in the rear, and fretted because his wound would not let him do his part.

The great victory won, it was agreed that Henry Ware had done the best of them all, but they spent little time in congratulations. They preferred the sacred duty of burying the dead, even seeking those who had fallen in the forest the night before; and then they began their march southward, the more severely wounded carried on rude litters at first, but as they gained strength after a while walking, though lamely. Paul recovered fast, and when he heard the story, he looked upon Henry as a knight, the equal of any who ever rode down the pages of chivalry.

But all alike carried in their hearts the consciousness that they had struck a mighty blow that would grant life to the growing settlements, and, despite their sadly thinned ranks, they were full of a pride that needed no words. The men of Wareville and the men of Marlowe parted at the appointed place, and then each force went home with the news of victory.

CHAPTER XVIII
THE TEST

THE people of Wareville had good reason alike for pride and for sorrow, pride for victory, and sorrow for the fallen, but they spent no time in either, at least openly, resuming at once the task of founding a new state.

Henry Ware, the hero of the hour and the savior of the village, laid aside his wild garb and took a place in his father's fields. The work was heavy, the Indian corn was planted, but trees were to be felled, fences were to be cut down, and as he was so strong a larger share than usual was expected of him. His own father appreciated these hopes and was resolved that his son should do his full duty.

Henry entered upon his task and from the beginning he had misgivings, but he refused to indulge them. He handled a hoe on his first day from dawn till dark in a hot field, and all the while the mighty wilderness about him was crying out to him in many voices. While the sun glowed upon him, and the sweat ran down his face he could see the deep cool shade of the forest--how restful and peaceful it looked there! He knew a sheltered glade where the buffalo were feeding, he could find the deer reposing in a thicket, and to the westward was a new region of hills and clear brooks, over which he might be the first white man to roam.

His blood tingled with his thoughts, but he never said a word, only bending lower to his task, and hardening his resolve. The voices of the wilderness might call, and he could not keep from hearing them, but he need not go. The amount of work he did that day was wonderful to all who saw, his vast strength put him far ahead of all others and back of his strength was his will. But they said nothing and he was glad they did not speak.

When he went home in the dusk he overtook Lucy Upton near the palisade. She was in the same red dress that she wore when she ran the gantlet and in the twilight it seemed to be tinged to a deeper scarlet. She was walking swiftly with the easy, swinging grace of a good figure and good health, but when he joined her she went more slowly.

He did not speak for a few moments, and she gave him a silent glance of sympathy. In her woman's heart she guessed the cause of his trouble, and while she had been afraid of him when he appeared suddenly as the Indian warrior yet she liked him better in that part than as she now saw him. Then he was majestic, now he was prosaic, and it seemed to her that his present role was unfitting.

"You are tired," she said at last.

"Well, not in the body exactly, but I feel like resting."

There was no complaint in his tone, but a slight touch of irony.

"Do you think that you will make a good farmer?" she asked.

"As good as the times and our situation allow," he replied. "Wandering parties of the savages are likely to pass near here and in the course of time they may send back an army. Besides one has to hunt now, as for a long while we must depend on the forest for a part of our food."

It seemed to her that these things did not cause him sorrow, that he turned to them as a sort of relief: his eyes sparkled more brightly when he spoke of the necessity for hunting and the possible passage of Indian parties which must be repelled. Girl though she was, she felt again a little glow of sympathy, guessing as she did his nature; she could understand how he thrilled when he heard the voices of the forest calling to him.

They reached the gate of the palisade and passed within. It was full dusk now, the forest blurring together into a mighty black wall, and the outlines of the houses becoming shadowy. The Ware family sat awhile that evening by the hearth fire, and John Ware was full of satisfaction. A worthy man, he had neither imagination nor primitive instincts and he valued the wilderness only as a cheap place in which to make homes. He spoke much of clearing the ground, of the great crops that would come, and of the profit and delight afforded by regular work year after year on the farm. Henry Ware sat in silence, listening to his father's oracular tones, but his mother, glancing at him, had doubts to which she gave no utterance.

The days passed and as the spring glided into summer they grew hotter. The sun glowed upon the fields, and the earth parched with thirst. In the forest the leaves were dry and they rustled when the wind blew upon them. The streams sank away again, as they had done during the siege, and labor became more trying. Yet Henry Ware never murmured, though his soul was full of black bitterness. Often he would resolutely turn his eyes from the forest where he knew the deep cool pools were, and keep them on the sun-baked field. His rifle, which had seemed to reproach him, inanimate object though it was, he hid in a corner of the house where he could not see it and its temptation. In order to create a counter-irritant he plunged into work with the most astonishing vigor.

John Ware, in those days, was full of pride and satisfaction, he rejoiced in the industrial prowess of his son, and he felt that his own influence had prevailed, he had led Henry back to the ways of civilization, the only right ways, and he enjoyed his triumph. But the schoolmaster, in secret, often shook his head.

The summer grew drier and hotter, it was a period of drought again and the little children gasped through the sweating nights. Afar they saw the blaze of forest fires and ashes and smoke came on the wind. Henry toiled with a dogged spirit, but every day the labor grew more bitter to him; he took no interest in it, he did not wish to calculate the result in the years to come, when all around him, extending thousands of miles, was an untrodden wilderness, in which he might roam and hunt until the end, although his years should be a hundred.

It was worst at night, when he lay awake by a window, breathing the hot air, then the deep cool forest extended to him her kindest invitation, and it took all his resolution to resist her welcome. The wind among the trees was like music, but it was a music to which he must close his ears. Then he remembered his vast wanderings with Black Cloud and his red friends, how they had crossed great and unnamed rivers, the days in the endless forest and the other days on the endless plains, and of the mighty lake they had reached in their northernmost journey--how cool and pleasant that lake seemed now! His mind ran over every detail of the great buffalo hunts, of those trips along the streams to trap the beaver and the events in the fight with the hostile tribe.

All these recollections seemed very vivid and real to him now, and the narrow life of Wareville faded into a mist out of which shone only the faces of those whom he loved--it was they alone who had brought him back to Wareville, but he knew that their ways were not his ways, and it was hard to confine his spirit within the narrow limits of a settlement.

But his long martyrdom went on, the summer was growing old, with the work of planting and cultivating almost done and the harvest soon to follow, and whatever his feelings may have been he had never flinched a single time. Nourished by his great labors the Ware farm far surpassed all others, and the pride of John Ware grew. He also grew more exacting with his pride, and this quality brought on the crisis.

Henry was building a fence one particularly hot afternoon, and his father coming by, cool and fresh, found fault with his work, chiefly to show his authority, because the work was not badly done--Mr. Ware was a good man, but like other good men he had a rare fault-finding impulse. The voices in the woods had been calling very loudly that day and Henry's temper suddenly flashed into a flame. But he did not give way to any external outburst of passion, speaking in a level, measured voice.

"I am sorry you do not like it," he said, "because it is the last work I am going to do here."

"Why--what do you mean?" exclaimed his father in astonishment.

"I am done," replied Henry in his firm tones, and dropping the fence rail that he held he walked to the house, every nerve in him thrilling with expectation of the pleasure that was to come. His mother was there, and she started in fear at his face.

"It is true, mother," he said, "I am not going to deceive you, I am going into the forest, but I will come again and often. It is the only life that I can lead, I was made for it I suppose; I have tried the other out there in the fields, and I have tried hard, but I cannot stand it."

She knew too well to seek to stop him. He took his rifle from its secluded corner, and the feeling of it, stock and barrel, was good to his hands. He put on the buckskin hunting shirt, leggings and moccasins, fringed and beaded, and with them he felt all his old zest and pride returning. He kissed his mother and sister good-by, shook hands with his younger brother, did the same with his astonished father at the door, and then, rifle on shoulder, disappeared in the circling forest.

That night Braxton Wyatt sneered and said that a savage could not keep from being a savage, but Paul Cotter turned upon him so fiercely that he took it back. The schoolmaster made no comment aloud, but to himself he said, "It was bound to come and perhaps it is no loss that it has come."

Meanwhile Henry Ware was tasting the fiercest and keenest joy of his life. The great forest seemed to reach out its boughs like kind arms to welcome and embrace. How cool was the shade! How the shafts of sunlight piercing the leaves fell like golden arrows on the ground! How the little brooks laughed and danced over the pebbles! This was his world and he had been too long away from it. Everything was friendly, the huge tree trunks were like old comrades, the air was fresher and keener than any that he had breathed in a long time, and was full of new life and zest. All his old wilderness love rushed back to him, and now after many months he felt at home.

Strong as he was already new strength flowed into his frame and he threw back his head, and laughed a low happy laugh. Then rifle at the trail he ran for miles among the trees from the pure happiness of living, but noting as he passed with wonderfully keen eyes every trail of a wild animal and all the forest signs that he knew so well. He ran many miles and he felt no weariness. Then he threw himself down on Mother Earth, and rejoiced at her embrace. He lay there a long time, staring up through the leaves and the shifting sunlight, and he was so still that a hare hopped through the undergrowth almost at his feet, never taking alarm. To Henry Ware then the world seemed grand and beautiful, and of all things in it God had made the wilderness the finest, lingering over every detail with a loving hand.

He watched the setting of the sun and the coming of the twilight. The sun was a great blazing ball and the western sky flowed away from it in circling waves of blue and pink and gold, then long shadows came over the forest, and the distant trees began to melt together into a gigantic dark wall. To the dweller in cities all this vast loneliness and desolation would have been dreary and weird beyond description; he would have shuddered with superstitious awe, starting in fear at the slightest sound, but there was no such quality in it for Henry Ware. He saw only comradeship and the friendly veil of the great creeping shadow. His eye could pierce the thickest night, and fear, either of the darkness or things physical, was not in him.

He rose after a while, when the last sign of day was gone, and walked on, though more slowly. He made no noise as he passed, stepping lightly, but with sure foot like one with both genius and training for the wilderness. He knelt at a little brook to slake his thirst, but did not stop long there. His happiness decreased in nowise. The familiar voices of the night were speaking to him. He heard the distant hoot of an owl, a deer rustled in the bush, a lizard scuttled over the leaves, and he rejoiced at the sounds. He did not think of hunger but toward midnight he raked some of last year's fallen leaves close to the trunk of a big tree, lay down upon them, and fell in a few moments into happy and dreamless sleep.

He awoke with the first rays of the dawn, shot a deer after an hour's search, and then cooked his breakfast by the side of one of the little brooks. It was the first food that had tasted just right to him in many weeks, and afterwards he lay by the camp fire awhile, and luxuriated. He had the most wonderful feeling of peace and ease; all the world was his to go where he chose and to do what he chose, and he began to think of an autumn camp, a tiny lodge in the deepest recess of the wilderness, where he could store spare ammunition, furs and skins and find a frequent refuge, when the time for storms and cold came. He would build at his ease--there was plenty of time and he would fill in the intervals with hunting and exploration.

He ranged that day toward the north and the west, moving with deliberation, and not until the third or the fourth day did he come to the place that he had in mind. In the triangle between the junction of two streams was a marshy area, thickly grown with bushes and slim trees, that thrust their roots deep down through the mire into more solid soil. The marsh was perhaps two acres in extent; right in the heart of it was a piece of firm earth about forty feet square and here Henry meant to build his lodge. He alone knew the path across the marsh over fallen logs lying near enough to each other to be reached by an agile man, and on the tiny island all his possessions would be safe.

He worked a week at his hut, and it was done, a little lean-to of bark and saplings, partly lined with skins, but proof against rain or snow. On the floor he spread the skins and furs of animals that he killed, and on the walls he hung trophies of the hunt.

Two weeks after his house was finished he used it at its full value. Summer was gone and autumn was coming, a great rain poured and the wind blew cold. Dead leaves fell in showers from the trees, and the boughs swaying before the gale creaked dismally against each other. But it all gave to Henry a supreme sense of physical comfort. He lay in his snug hut, and, pulling a little to one side the heavy buffalo robe that hung over the doorway, watched the storm rage through the wilderness. He had no sense of loneliness, his mind was in perfect tune with everything about him, and delighted in the triumphant manifestation of nature.

He stayed there all day, content to lie still and meditate vaguely of anything that came of its own accord into his mind. About the twilight hour he cooked some venison, ate it and then slept a dreamless sleep through the night.

The rain ceased the next day but the air became crisp and cold, and autumn was fully come. In a week the forest was dyed into the most glowing colors, red and yellow and brown, and the shades between. The heavens were pure blue and gold, and it was a poignant delight to breathe the keen air. Again he ranged far and rejoiced in the hunting. His infallible rifle never missed, and in the little hut in the marsh the stock of furs and skins grew so fast that scarcely room for himself was left. He hid a fresh store at another place in the forest, and then he returned to Wareville for a day. His father greeted him with some constraint, not with coldness exactly, but with lack of understanding. His mother and his sister wept with joy and Mrs. Ware said: "I was expecting you about this time and you have not disappointed me."

He stayed two days and his keen eyes, so observant of material matters, noted that the colony was not doing well for the time, the drought having almost ruined the crops and there was full promise of scanty food and a hard winter. Now came his opportunity. He had looked upon his month in the forest as in part a holiday, and he never intended to throw aside all responsibility for others, roving the wilderness absolutely free from care. He knew that he would have work to do, he felt that he should have it, and now he saw the way to do the kind of work that he loved to do.

He replenished his supply of ammunition, took up his rifle again and returned to the forest. Now he used all his surpassing knowledge and skill in the chase, and game began to pour into the colony, bear, deer, buffalo and the smaller animals, until he alone seemed able to feed the entire settlement through the winter.

He experienced a new thrill keener and more delightful than any that had gone before; he was doing for others and the knowledge was most pleasant. Winter came on, fierce and unyielding with almost continuous snow and ice, and Henry Ware was the chief support of that little village in the wilderness. The game wandering with its fancy, or perhaps taking alarm at the new settlement had drifted far, and he alone of all the hunters could find it. The voices that had been raised against him a second time were stilled again, because no one dared to accuse when his single figure stood between them and starvation.

He took Paul Cotter with him on some of his hunts, but never even to Paul did he tell the secret of his hut in the morass; that was to be guarded for himself alone. He was fond of Paul, but Paul able though he was fell far behind Henry in the forest.

The debt of Wareville to him grew and none felt privileged to criticise him now, as he appeared from the forest and disappeared into it again on his self-chosen tasks.

The winter broke up at last, but with the spring came a new and more formidable danger. Small parties of Indians, not strong enough to attack Wareville itself but sufficient for forest ambush, began to appear in the country, and two or three lives that could be ill spared were lost. Now Henry Ware showed his supreme value; he was a match and more than a match for the savages at all their own tricks, and he became the ranger for the settlement, its champion against a wild and treacherous foe.

The tales of his skill and prowess spread far through the wilderness. Single handed he would not hesitate in the depths of the forest to attack war parties of half a dozen, and while suffering heavily themselves they could never catch their daring tormentor. These tales even spread across the Ohio to the Indian villages, where they told of a blond and giant white youth in the South who was the spirit of death, whom no runner could overtake, whom no bullet could slay and who raged against the red man with an invincible wrath.

As his single hand had fed them through the winter so his single hand protected them from death in the spring. He seemed to know by instinct when the war parties were coming and where they would appear. Always he confronted them with some devious attack that they did not know how to meet, and Wareville remained inviolate.

Then, in the summer, when the war bands were all gone he came back to Wareville to stay a while, although, everyone, himself included, knew that he would always remain a son of the wilderness, spending but part of his time in the houses of men.

CHAPTER XIX
AN ERRAND AND A FRIEND

TWO stalwart lads were marching steadily through the deep woods, some months later. They were boys in years, but in size, strength, alertness and knowledge of the forest far beyond their age. One, in particular, would have drawn the immediate and admiring glance of every keen-eyed frontiersman, so powerful was he, and yet so light and quick of movement. His wary glance seemed to read every secret of tree, bush and grass, and his head, crowned by a great mass of thick, yellow hair, rose several inches above that of his comrade, who would have been called by most people a tall boy.

The two youths were dressed almost alike. Each wore a cap of raccoon fur, with the short tail hanging from the back of it as a decoration. Their bodies were clad in hunting shirts, made of the skin of the deer, softly and beautifully tanned and dyed green. The fine fringe of the shirt hung almost to the knees, and below it were leggings also of deerskin, beaded at the seams. The feet were inclosed in deerskin moccasins, fitting tightly, but very soft and light. A rifle, a tomahawk, and a useful knife at the belt completed the equipment.

They were walking, but each boy led a stout horse, and on the back of this horse was a great brown sack that hung down, puffy, on either side. The sacks were filled with gunpowder made from cave-dust and the two boys, Henry Ware and Paul Cotter, were carrying it to a distant village that had exhausted its supply, but which, hearing of the strange new way in which Wareville obtained it, had sent begging for a loan of this commodity, more precious to the pioneer than gold and jewels. The response was quick and spontaneous and Henry and Paul had been chosen to take the powder, an errand in which both rejoiced. Already they had been two days in the great wilderness, now painted in gorgeous colors by the hand of autumn, and they had not seen a sign of a human being, white or red.

They walked steadily on, and the trained horses followed, each just behind his master, although there was no hand upon the bridle. They stopped presently at the low rounded crest of a hill, where the forest opened out a little, and, as if with the same impulse, each looked off toward the vast horizon with a glowing eye. The mighty forest, vivid with its gleaming reds and yellows and browns, rolled away for miles, and then died to the eye where the silky blue arch of the sky came down to meet it. Now and then there was a flash of silver, where a brook ran between the hills, and the wind brought an air, crisp, fresh and full of life.

It was beautiful, this great wilderness of Kaintuckee, and each boy saw it according to his nature. Henry, the soul of action, the boy of the keen senses and the mighty physical nature, loved it for its own sake and for what it was in the present. He fitted into it and was a part of it. The towns and the old civilization in the east never called to him. He had found the place that nature intended for him. He was here the wilderness rover, hunter and scout, the border champion and defender, the primitive founder of a state, without whom, and his like, our Union could never have been built up. Henry gloried in the wilderness and loved its life which was so easy to him. Paul, the boy of thought, was always looking into the future, and already he foresaw what would come to pass in a later generation.

Neither spoke, and presently, by the same impulse, they started on again, descending the low hill, and plunging once more into the forest. When they had gone about half a mile, Henry stopped suddenly. His wonderful physical organism, as sensitive as the machinery of a watch, had sounded an alarm. A faint sound, not much more than the fall of a dying leaf, came to his ears and he knew at once that it was not a natural noise of the forest. He held up his hand and stopped, and Paul, who trusted him implicitly, stopped also. Henry listened intently with ears that heard everything, and the sound came to him again. It was a footfall. A human being, besides themselves, was near in the forest!

"Come, Paul," he said, and he began to creep toward the sound, the two darting from tree to tree, and making no noise among the fallen leaves, as they brushed past, with their soft moccasins. The trained horses remained where they had been left, silent and motionless.

Henry, as was natural, was in front, and he was the first to see the object that had caused the noise. A man stepped from the shelter of a tree's great trunk, and, although armed, he held up one hand, in the manner of a friend. He was an Indian of middle age and dignified look, although he was not painted like any of the tribes that came down to make war in Kentucky.

Henry recognized at once the friendly signal, and he too stepped from the cover of the forest, walking slowly toward the warrior, who was undoubtedly a chief and a man of importance. Twenty feet away, the boy started a little, and a sudden light leaped into his eyes. Then he strode up rapidly, and took the warrior's hand after the white custom.

"Black Cloud! My friend!" he said.

"You know me! You have not forgotten?" replied the chief and his eyes gleamed ever so quickly.

"You have come far from your people and among hostile tribes to see me?" said Henry who instantly divined the truth.

"It is so," replied the chief, "and to ask you to go back with me. Our warriors miss you."

Henry was moved to the depths of his nature. Black Cloud had come a thousand miles to ask him this question, and he had a far, sweet vision of a life utterly wild and free. Again he saw the great plains, and again came to his ears, like rolling thunder, the tread of the myriad-footed buffalo herd. He was tempted sorely tempted and he knew it, but, with a mighty effort he put the temptation away from him and shook his head.

"It cannot be, Black Cloud," he said. "My people need me, as yours need you."

A shadow passed over the eyes of the chief, but it was gone in a moment. He knew that the answer was final, and he said not another word on the subject.

Black Cloud went on with Henry and Paul half a day, then he bade them farewell. They watched him go, but it could be only for a minute or two, because his form quickly melted away into the forest. Then the two boys, turning their faces steadily toward duty, marched on, and the great wilderness, gleaming in its reds and yellows and browns curved about them.

THE END

The Two Babylons
Alexander Hislop
You may be surprised to learn that many traditions of Roman Catholicism in fact don't come from Christ's teachings but from an ancient Babylonian "Mystery" religion that was centered on Nimrod, his wife Semiramis, and a child Tammuz. This book shows how this ancient religion transformed itself as it incorporated Christ into its teachings....

Religion/History   **Pages:358**

ISBN: *1-59462-010-5*   **MSRP** *$22.95*

The Power Of Concentration
Theron Q. Dumont
It is of the utmost value to learn how to concentrate. To make the greatest success of anything you must be able to concentrate your entire thought upon the idea you are working on. The person that is able to concentrate utilizes all constructive thoughts and shuts out all destructive ones...

Self Help/Inspirational   **Pages:196**

ISBN: *1-59462-141-1*   **MSRP** *$14.95*

Rightly Dividing The Word
Clarence Larkin
The "Fundamental Doctrines" of the Christian Faith are clearly outlined in numerous books on Theology, but they are not available to the average reader and were mainly written for students. The Author has made it the work of his ministry to preach the "Fundamental Doctrines." To this end he has aimed to express them in the simplest and clearest manner..

Religion   **Pages:352**

ISBN: *1-59462-334-1*   **MSRP** *$23.45*

The Law of Psychic Phenomena
Thomson Jay Hudson
"I do not expect this book to stand upon its literary merits; for if it is unsound in principle, felicity of diction cannot save it, and if sound, homeliness of expression cannot destroy it. My primary object in offering it to the public is to assist in bringing Psychology within the domain of the exact sciences. That this has never been accomplished..."

New Age   **Pages:420**

ISBN: *1-59462-124-1*   **MSRP** *$29.95*

Beautiful Joe
Marshall Saunders
When Marshall visited the Moore family in 1892, she discovered Joe, a dog they had nursed back to health from his previous abusive home to live a happy life. So moved was she, that she wrote this classic masterpiece which won accolades and was recognized as a heartwarming symbol for humane animal treatment...

Fiction   **Pages:256**

ISBN: *1-59462-261-2*   **MSRP** *$18.45*

The Codes Of Hammurabi And Moses - W. W. Davies
The discovery of the Hammurabi Code is one of the greatest achievements of archaeology, and is of paramount interest, not only to the student of the Bible, but also to all those interested in ancient history...

Religion   **Pages:132**

ISBN: *1-59462-338-4*   **MSRP** *$12.95*

The Thirty-Six Dramatic Situations
Georges Polti
An incredibly useful guide for aspiring authors and playwrights. This volume categorizes every dramatic situation which could occur in a story and describes them in a list of 36 situations. A great aid to help inspire or formalize the creative writing process...

Self Help/Reference   **Pages:204**

ISBN: *1-59462-134-9*   **MSRP** *$15.95*

The Go-Getter
Kyne B. Peter
The Go Getter is the story of William Peck.He was a war veteran and amputee who will not be refused what he wants. Peck not only fights to find employment but continually proves himself more than competent at the many difficult test that are throw his way in the course of his early days with the Ricks Lumber Company...

Business/Self Help/Inspirational   **Pages:68**

ISBN: *1-59462-186-1*   **MSRP** *$8.95*

Self Mastery
Emile Coue
Emile Coue came up with novel way to improve the lives of people. He was a pharmacist by trade and often saw ailing people. This lead him to develop autosuggestion, a form of self-hypnosis. At the time his theories weren't popular but over the years evidence is mounting that he was indeed right all along...

New Age/Self Help   **Pages:98**

ISBN: *1-59462-189-6*   **MSRP** *$7.95*

The Awful Disclosures Of Maria Monk
"I cannot banish the scenes and characters of this book from my memory. To me it can never appear like an amusing fable, or lose its interest and importance. The story is one which is continually before me, and must return fresh to my mind with painful emotions as long as I live..."

Religion   **Pages:232**

ISBN: *1-59462-160-8*   **MSRP** *$17.95*

As a Man Thinketh
James Allen
"This little volume (the result of meditation and experience) is not intended as an exhaustive treatise on the much-written-upon subject of the power of thought. It is suggestive rather than explanatory, its object being to stimulate men and women to the discovery and perception of the truth that by virtue of the thoughts which they choose and encourage..."

Inspirational/Self Help   **Pages:80**

ISBN: *1-59462-231-0*   **MSRP** *$9.45*

The Enchanted April
Elizabeth Von Arnim
It began in a woman's club in London on a February afternoon, an uncomfortable club, and a miserable afternoon when Mrs. Wilkins, who had come down from Hampstead to shop and had lunched at her club, took up The Times from the table in the smoking-room...

Fiction   **Pages:368**

ISBN: *1-59462-150-0*   **MSRP** *$23.45*

Holland - The History Of Netherlands
Thomas Colley Grattan
Thomas Grattan was a prestigious writer from Dublin who served as British Consul to the US. Among his works is an authoritative look at the history of Holland. A colorful and interesting look at history....

History/Politics   **Pages:408**

ISBN: *1-59462-137-3*   **MSRP** *$26.95*

A Concise Dictionary of Middle English
A. L. Mayhew
Walter W. Skeat
The present work is intended to meet, in some measure, the requirements of those who wish to make some study of Middle-English, and who find a difficulty in obtaining such assistance as will enable them to find out the meanings and etymologies of the words most essential to their purpose...

Reference/History   **Pages:332**

ISBN: *1-59462-119-5*   **MSRP** *$29.95*

The Witch-Cult in Western Europe
Margaret Murray
QTY

The mass of existing material on this subject is so great that I have not attempted to make a survey of the whole of European "Witchcraft" but have confined myself to an intensive study of the cult in Great Britain. In order, however, to obtain a clearer understanding of the ritual and beliefs I have had recourse to French and Flemish sources...

Occult   **Pages:308**

ISBN: *1-59462-126-8*   **MSRP** *$22.45*

The Science Of Psychic Healing
Yogi Ramacharaka

This book is not a book of theories it deals with facts. Its author regards the best of theories as but working hypotheses to be used only until better ones present themselves. The "fact" is the principal thing the essential thing to uncover which the tool, theory, is used...

New Age/Health   **Pages:180**

ISBN: *1-59462-140-3*   **MSRP** *$13.95*

Bible Myths
Thomas Doane

In pursuing the study of the Bible Myths, facts pertaining thereto, in a condensed form, seemed to be greatly needed, and nowhere to be found. Widely scattered through hundreds of ancient and modern volumes, most of the contents of this book may indeed be found; but any previous attempt to trace exclusively the myths and legends...

Religion/History   **Pages:644**

ISBN: *1-59462-163-2*   **MSRP** *$38.95*

Tertium Organum
P. D. Ouspensky

A truly mind expanding writing that combines science with mysticism with unprecedented elegance. He presents the world we live in as a multi dimensional world and time as a motion through this world. But this isn't a cold and purely analytical explanation but a masterful presentation filled with similes and analogies...

New Age   **Pages:356**

ISBN: *1-59462-205-1*   **MSRP** *$23.95*

Advance Course in Yogi Philosophy
Yogi Ramacharaka

"The twelve lessons forming this volume were originally issued in the shape of monthly lessons, known as "The Advanced Course in Yogi Philosophy and Oriental Occultism" during a period of twelve months beginning with October, 1904, and ending September, 1905."

Philosophy/Inspirational/Self Help   Pages:340

ISBN: *1-59462-229-9*   **MSRP** *$22.95*

Ambassador Morgenthau's Story
Henry Morgenthau

"By this time the American people have probably become convinced that the Germans deliberately planned the conquest of the world. Yet they hesitate to convict on circumstantial evidence and for this reason all eye witnesses to this, the greatest crime in modern history, should volunteer their testimony..."

History   **Pages:472**

ISBN: *1-59462-244-2*   **MSRP** *$29.95*

The Aquarian Gospel of Jesus the Christ
Levi Dowling

A retelling of Jesus' story which tells us what happened during the twenty year gap left by the Bible's New Testament. It tells of his travels to the far-east where he studied with the masters and fought against the rigid caste system. This book has enjoyed a resurgence in modern America and provides spiritual insight with charm. Its influences can be seen throughout the Age of Aquarius.

Religion   **Pages:264**

ISBN: *1-59462-321-X*   **MSRP** *$18.95*

Philosophy Of Natural Therapeutics
Henry Lindlahr
QTY

We invite the earnest cooperation in this great work of all those who have awakened to the necessity for more rational living and for radical reform in healing methods...

Health/Philosophy/Self Help   Pages:552

ISBN: *1-59462-132-2*   **MSRP** *$34.95*

A Message to Garcia
Elbert Hubbard

This literary trifle, A Message to Garcia, was written one evening after supper, in a single hour. It was on the Twenty-second of February, Eighteen Hundred Ninety-nine, Washington's Birthday, and we were just going to press with the March Philistine...

New Age/Fiction   **Pages:92**

ISBN: *1-59462-144-6*   **MSRP** *$9.95*

The Book of Jasher
Alcuinus Flaccus Albinus

The Book of Jasher is an historical religious volume that many consider as a missing holy book from the Old Testament. Particularly studied by the Church of Later Day Saints and historians, it covers the history of the world from creation until the period of Judges in Israel. It's authenticity is bolstered due to a reference to the Book of Jasher in the Bible in Joshua 10:13

Religion/History   **Pages:276**

ISBN: *1-59462-197-7*   **MSRP** *$18.95*

The Titan
Theodore Dreiser

"When Frank Algernon Cowperwood emerged from the Eastern District Penitentiary, in Philadelphia he realized that the old life he had lived in that city since boyhood was ended. His youth was gone, and with it had been lost the great business prospects of his earlier manhood. He must begin again..."

Fiction   **Pages:564**

ISBN: *1-59462-220-5*   **MSRP** *$33.95*

Biblical Essays
J. B. Lightfoot

About one-third of the present volume has already seen the light. The opening essay "On the Internal Evidence for the Authenticity and Genuineness of St John's Gospel" was published in the "Expositor" in the early months of 1890, and has been reprinted since...

Religion/History   **Pages:480**

ISBN: *1-59462-238-8*   **MSRP** *$30.95*

The Settlement Cook Book
Simon Kander

A legacy from the civil war, this book is a classic "American charity cookbook," which was used for fundraisers starting in Milwaukee. While it has transformed over the years, this printing provides great recipes from American history. Over two million copies have been sold. This volume contains a rich collection of recipes from noted chefs and hostesses of the turn of the century...

How-to   **Pages:472**

ISBN: *1-59462-256-6*   **MSRP** *$29.95*

My Life and Work
Henry Ford

Henry Ford revolutionized the world with his implementation of mass production for the Model T automobile. Gain valuable business insight into his life and work with his own auto-biography... "We have only started on our development of our country we have not as yet, with all our talk of wonderful progress, done more than scratch the surface. The progress has been wonderful enough but..."

Biographies/History/Business   Pages:300

ISBN: *1-59462-198-5*   **MSRP** *$21.95*

QTY

☐ **The Rosicrucian Cosmo-Conception Mystic Christianity** *by Max Heindel*   ISBN: *1-59462-188-8* **$38.95**
The Rosicrucian Cosmo-conception is not dogmatic, neither does it appeal to any other authority than the reason of the student. It is: not controversial, but is: sent forth in the, hope that it may help to clear...   New Age/Religion Pages 646

☐ **Abandonment To Divine Providence** *by Jean-Pierre de Caussade*   ISBN: *1-59462-228-0* **$25.95**
"The Rev. Jean Pierre de Caussade was one of the most remarkable spiritual writers of the Society of Jesus in France in the 18th Century. His death took place at Toulouse in 1751. His works have gone through many editions and have been republished...   Inspirational/Religion Pages 400

☐ **Mental Chemistry** *by Charles Haanel*   ISBN: *1-59462-192-6* **$23.95**
Mental Chemistry allows the change of material conditions by combining and appropriately utilizing the power of the mind. Much like applied chemistry creates something new and unique out of careful combinations of chemicals the mastery of mental chemistry...   New Age Pages 354

☐ **The Letters of Robert Browning and Elizabeth Barret Barrett 1845-1846 vol II**   ISBN: *1-59462-193-4* **$35.95**
by Robert Browning and Elizabeth Barrett   Biographies Pages 596

☐ **Gleanings In Genesis (volume I)** *by Arthur W. Pink*   ISBN: *1-59462-130-6* **$27.45**
Appropriately has Genesis been termed "the seed plot of the Bible" for in it we have, in germ form, almost all of the great doctrines which are afterwards fully developed in the books of Scripture which follow...   Religion/Inspirational Pages 420

☐ **The Master Key** *by L. W. de Laurence*   ISBN: *1-59462-001-6* **$30.95**
In no branch of human knowledge has there been a more lively increase of the spirit of research during the past few years than in the study of Psychology, Concentration and Mental Discipline. The requests for authentic lessons in Thought Control, Mental Discipline and...   New Age/Business Pages 422

☐ **The Lesser Key Of Solomon Goetia** *by L. W. de Laurence*   ISBN: *1-59462-092-X* **$9.95**
This translation of the first book of the "Lemegton" which is now for the first time made accessible to students of Talismanic Magic was done, after careful collation and edition, from numerous Ancient Manuscripts in Hebrew, Latin, and French...   New Age/Occult Pages 92

☐ **Rubaiyat Of Omar Khayyam** *by Edward Fitzgerald*   ISBN: *1-59462-332-5* **$13.95**
Edward Fitzgerald, whom the world has already learned, in spite of his own efforts to remain within the shadow of anonymity, to look upon as one of the rarest poets of the century, was born at Bredfield, in Suffolk, on the 31st of March, 1809. He was the third son of John Purcell...   Music Pages 172

☐ **Ancient Law** *by Henry Maine*   ISBN: *1-59462-128-4* **$29.95**
The chief object of the following pages is to indicate some of the earliest ideas of mankind, as they are reflected in Ancient Law, and to point out the relation of those ideas to modern thought.   Religion/History Pages 452

☐ **Far-Away Stories** *by William J. Locke*   ISBN: *1-59462-129-2* **$19.45**
"Good wine needs no bush, but a collection of mixed vintages does. And this book is just such a collection. Some of the stories I do not want to remain buried for ever in the museum files of dead magazine-numbers an author's not unpardonable vanity..."   Fiction Pages 272

☐ **Life of David Crockett** *by David Crockett*   ISBN: *1-59462-250-7* **$27.45**
"Colonel David Crockett was one of the most remarkable men of the times in which he lived. Born in humble life, but gifted with a strong will, an indomitable courage, and unremitting perseverance...   Biographies/New Age Pages 424

☐ **Lip-Reading** *by Edward Nitchie*   ISBN: *1-59462-206-X* **$25.95**
Edward B. Nitchie, founder of the New York School for the Hard of Hearing, now the Nitchie School of Lip-Reading, Inc, wrote "LIP-READING Principles and Practice". The development and perfecting of this meritorious work on lip-reading was an undertaking...   How-to Pages 400

☐ **A Handbook of Suggestive Therapeutics, Applied Hypnotism, Psychic Science**   ISBN: *1-59462-214-0* **$24.95**
by Henry Munro   Health/New Age/Health/Self-help Pages 376

☐ **A Doll's House: and Two Other Plays** *by Henrik Ibsen*   ISBN: *1-59462-112-8* **$19.95**
Henrik Ibsen created this classic when in revolutionary 1848 Rome. Introducing some striking concepts in playwriting for the realist genre, this play has been studied the world over.   Fiction/Classics/Plays 308

☐ **The Light of Asia** *by sir Edwin Arnold*   ISBN: *1-59462-204-3* **$13.95**
In this poetic masterpiece, Edwin Arnold describes the life and teachings of Buddha. The man who was to become known as Buddha to the world was born as Prince Gautama of India but he rejected the worldly riches and abandoned the reigns of power when...   Religion/History/Biographies Pages 170

☐ **The Complete Works of Guy de Maupassant** *by Guy de Maupassant*   ISBN: *1-59462-157-8* **$16.95**
"For days and days, nights and nights, I had dreamed of that first kiss which was to consecrate our engagement, and I knew not on what spot I should put my lips..."   Fiction/Classics Pages 240

☐ **The Art of Cross-Examination** *by Francis L. Wellman*   ISBN: *1-59462-309-0* **$26.95**
Written by a renowned trial lawyer, Wellman imparts his experience and uses case studies to explain how to use psychology to extract desired information through questioning.   How-to/Science/Reference Pages 408

☐ **Answered or Unanswered?** *by Louisa Vaughan*   ISBN: *1-59462-248-5* **$10.95**
Miracles of Faith in China   Religion Pages 112

☐ **The Edinburgh Lectures on Mental Science (1909)** *by Thomas*   ISBN: *1-59462-008-3* **$11.95**
This book contains the substance of a course of lectures recently given by the writer in the Queen Street Hall, Edinburgh. Its purpose is to indicate the Natural Principles governing the relation between Mental Action and Material Conditions...   New Age/Psychology Pages 148

☐ **Ayesha** *by H. Rider Haggard*   ISBN: *1-59462-301-5* **$24.95**
Verily and indeed it is the unexpected that happens! Probably if there was one person upon the earth from whom the Editor of this, and of a certain previous history, did not expect to hear again...   Classics Pages 380

☐ **Ayala's Angel** *by Anthony Trollope*   ISBN: *1-59462-352-X* **$29.95**
The two girls were both pretty; but Lucy who was twenty-one who supposed to be simple and comparatively unattractive, whereas Ayala was credited, as her Bombwhat romantic name might show, with poetic charm and a taste for romance. Ayala when her father died was nineteen...   Fiction Pages 484

☐ **The American Commonwealth** *by James Bryce*   ISBN: *1-59462-286-8* **$34.45**
An interpretation of American democratic political theory. It examines political mechanics and society from the perspective of Scotsman James Bryce   Politics Pages 572

☐ **Stories of the Pilgrims** *by Margaret P. Pumphrey*   ISBN: *1-59462-116-0* **$17.95**
This book explores pilgrims religious oppression in England as well as their escape to Holland and eventual crossing to America on the Mayflower, and their early days in New England...   History Pages 268

www.bookjungle.com *email: sales@bookjungle.com fax: 630-214-0564 mail: Book Jungle PO Box 2226 Champaign, IL 61825*

QTY

The Fasting Cure by **Sinclair Upton**　　ISBN: *1-59462-222-1*　**$13.95**
In the Cosmopolitan Magazine for May, 1910, and in the Contemporary Review (London) for April, 1910, I published an article dealing with my experiences in fasting. I have written a great many magazine articles, but never one which attracted so much attention... New Age/Self Help/Health Pages 164

Hebrew Astrology by **Sepharial**　　ISBN: *1-59462-308-2*　**$13.45**
In these days of advanced thinking it is a matter of common observation that we have left many of the old landmarks behind and that we are now pressing forward to greater heights and to a wider horizon than that which represented the mind-content of our progenitors... Astrology Pages 144

Thought Vibration or The Law of Attraction in the Thought World　ISBN: *1-59462-127-6*　**$12.95**

by **William Walker Atkinson**　　Psychology/Religion Pages 144

Optimism by **Helen Keller**　　ISBN: *1-59462-108-X*　**$15.95**
Helen Keller was blind, deaf, and mute since 19 months old, yet famously learned how to overcome these handicaps, communicate with the world, and spread her lectures promoting optimism. An inspiring read for everyone... Biographies/Inspirational Pages 84

Sara Crewe by **Frances Burnett**　　ISBN: *1-59462-360-0*　**$9.45**
In the first place, Miss Minchin lived in London. Her home was a large, dull, tall one, in a large, dull square, where all the houses were alike, and all the sparrows were alike, and where all the door-knockers made the same heavy sound... Childrens/Classic Pages 88

The Autobiography of Benjamin Franklin by **Benjamin Franklin**　　ISBN: *1-59462-135-7*　**$24.95**
The Autobiography of Benjamin Franklin has probably been more extensively read than any other American historical work, and no other book of its kind has had such ups and downs of fortune. Franklin lived for many years in England, where he was agent... Biographies/History Pages 332

Name	
Email	
Telephone	
Address	
City, State ZIP	

☐ **Credit Card**　　　☐ **Check / Money Order**

Credit Card Number	
Expiration Date	
Signature	

Please Mail to:　Book Jungle
PO Box 2226
Champaign, IL 61825
or Fax to:　　630-214-0564

ORDERING INFORMATION

web*: www.bookjungle.com*
email*: sales@bookjungle.com*
fax*: 630-214-0564*
mail*: Book Jungle PO Box 2226 Champaign, IL 61825*
or PayPal *to sales@bookjungle.com*

Please contact us for bulk discounts

DIRECT-ORDER TERMS

20% Discount if You Order
Two or More Books
Free Domestic Shipping!
Accepted: Master Card, Visa,
Discover, American Express

Printed in the United States
216969BV00003B/2/A

9 781604 240313